Contents

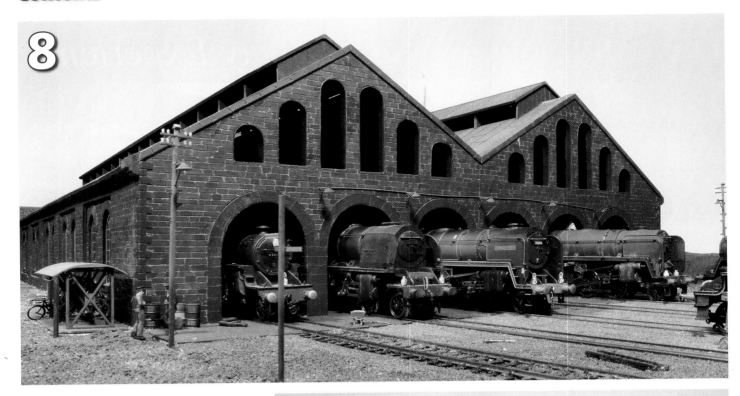

8

14

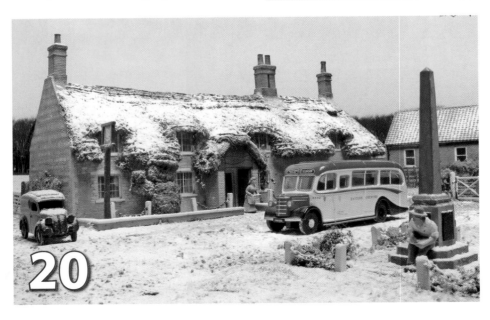

20

One of our project layouts this year has been based on the Wisbech & Upwell Tramway, always a popular subject with modellers. You can see this starter layout at our shows during 2013 and there will be a chance for readers to win it in a competition later in the year. Tom Mattingley

Welcome to the 2013 BRM Annual

This year, *British Railway Modelling* enters its twentieth year of publication, not bad for what was seen as a 'new kid on the block' back in 1993. In that year Ford unveiled the Mondeo, Bill Clinton became President of the United States, and the internet was born when CERN announced that their 'World Wide Web' was free to all to use without any fees. The first high speed test train ran through the new channel tunnel, and the Railways Act (1993) paved the way for rail privatisation.

Until then the model railway press had been a mostly black and white world - 'soot and whitewash' as Tony Wright called it. Edited by David Brown, *BRM* combined the latest print and publishing technology with the high standards of modelling in the country. Two decades later, I hope readers will see that we have not stood still but are once again at the forefront of publishing technology, although new developments centre around electronic publishing with BRM available in digital form

for phones, computers and tablets.

With a spate of third rail Southern electric units being released by our two major manufacturers, we have a Southern Region theme to this year's annual. In 'Third Rail and Semaphores' Graeme Elgar remembers the last days of the 2-EPBs, while Gerrard Futtrell looks at Addiscombe and Martin Axford considers Hayes as suitable third rail layout projects. Andy Hopper builds a resin 2-HAL and we revisit Oxminster to see developments on this OO gauge Southern Region system.

Elsewhere we visit Annan Road shed, John Cockcroft describes construction of a Furness Railway 'Seagull', and Graham Nicholas introduces his 4mm recreation of Grantham. There's also a slice of 1950s nostalgia with Grantley - Peter's layout - and Tony Wright shows how he replaced the tender drive of several older 4mm locos with up to date chassis and mechanisms.

As always, there's plenty to read so until next time - Happy Modelling!

[signature]

BRITISH RAILWAY MODELLING ANNUAL 2013

British Railway Modelling Annual 2013 is published by Warners Group Publications plc
Tel: 01778 392455 Fax: 01778 425437

PUBLISHER
John Greenwood
johng@warnersgroup.co.uk

EDITORIAL
Brand Editor
Steve Cole
stevec@warnersgroup.co.uk
Editor
John Emerson
johne@warnersgroup.co.uk
Editorial Assistant
Richard Wilson 01778 392455
richardw@warnersgroup.co.uk
Staff Writer
Howard Smith 01778 392059
howards@warnersgroup.co.uk
Diary Dates Secretary
Katie Phillips 01778 391104
katiep@warnersgroup.co.uk
RMweb/Modelling Inspiration Editor
Andy York
info@rmweb.co.uk
Track Plan Illustrator
Ian Wilson at Pacific Studio
ian@pacificstudio.co.uk

ADVERTISING
Group Advertising Manager
Bev Francis 01778 392055
bevf@warnersgroup.co.uk
Advertising
Judy Stevens 01778 395002
judys@warnersgroup.co.uk

DESIGN AND PRODUCTION
Senior Designer
Andy Fletcher
andrewf@warnersgroup.co.uk
Advert Design
Becky Duffy, Amie Carter
beckyd@warnersgroup.co.uk
amiec@warnersgroup.co.uk
Production
Pat Price 01778 391115
patp@warnersgroup.co.uk

SUBSCRIPTIONS
01778 392002

DISTRIBUTION
Trade Account Sales
Natalie Cole 01778 392404
Vicky Courton 01778 391150
tradeaccountorders @warnersgroup.co.uk
UK/Overseas Newstrade Sales
Andrew Stark 01778 391194
andrews@warnersgroup.co.uk
Newstrade Distribution
Tom Brown 01778 391135
ISSN 0968-0764

PRINTING
Warners (Midlands) plc, The Maltings, West Street, Bourne, Lincolnshire PE10 9PH

Ideas for future contributions should be sent in outline form to the Editor for consideration. Please clearly mark all material with your name and address, and include sufficient postage if you require material to be returned. Views expressed by contributors are not necessarily those of the Editor or Publisher. From time to time Warners may lend reputable companies the names and addresses of readers who have responded to offers, services and competitions organised by BRM. If you do not wish to receive such mailings, please write to Warners Group Distribution, Dept WD, Manor Lane, Bourne, Lincolnshire PE10 9PH or call 01778 391153.

ANNAN ROAD

Spencer Anderson from East Kilbride MRC describes their OO gauge shed-based exhibition layout. *Photography by Tony Wright.*

Starting on any new major project for East Kilbride MRC is a decision which has to be considered and discussed in some detail and for some time before a final choice is made. The onset of these actions started back in 2008 when it was decided to build an OO gauge MPD layout.

The original concept was to have a scenic section comprising three baseboards with the MPD and servicing facilities with main line to the front and two small traverser boards - one at each end – to allow for short train workings. The main object of the layout was to create a working shed – the question being which one? Dumfries on the former Glasgow & South Western seemed to be the obvious choice as it ticked all the right boxes. We could do it (with certain compromises) in the limited space we had available to us in our clubrooms and as a few club members have BR motive power the period set was during the final years of British steam.

The first three baseboards were designed and built to accommodate the shed, the road which divides the shed from the servicing facilities and the long graceful curve of the main line. The main lines are laid onto cork underlay and the remainder of the track is laid directly on to the baseboards. Trackwork is Peco code 75 with large radius live frog points operated by Fulgurex point motors. The turntable we opted for was the Heljan 89011 – a fine model which has performed well.

A new method of construction was tried out with a framework being built onto which the baseboards would simply sit. It was felt that although this did work it was not pursued for the rest of the layout - more of which later.

As the layout (now called Annan Road – after the road which crosses the railway) progressed, it was decided that to do the shed justice it would have to become a continuous run layout to allow scale length trains to run with frequent changes of locomotives taking place.

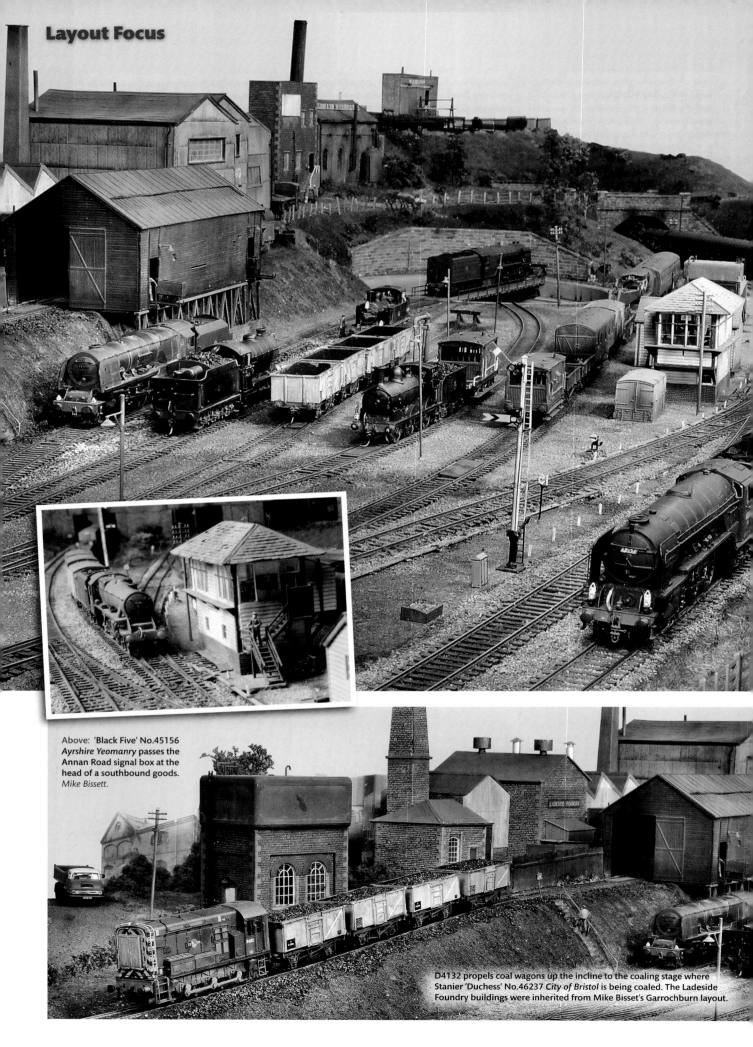

Above: 'Black Five' No.45156 *Ayrshire Yeomanry* passes the Annan Road signal box at the head of a southbound goods. *Mike Bissett.*

D4132 propels coal wagons up the incline to the coaling stage where Stanier 'Duchess' No.46237 *City of Bristol* is being coaled. The Ladeside Foundry buildings were inherited from Mike Bisset's Garrochburn layout.

A1 No.60134 heads a Down express past an unidentified sister engine on the turntable. 46237 *City of Bristol*, a Caley 'Jumbo' and two other unidentified engines are also visible. The breakdown train is parked in its siding.

A1 No.60164 *Robert Reekie* (modellers licence) thunders past the scrapyard on a northbound express. *Mike Bissett*.

A variety of locos can be seen at the servicing facilities including ex-Caley 'Jumbo' No.57389, 'Duchess' No.46237 *City of Bristol*, J36 No.64836 and an unidentified 'Jinty'. The breakdown train can be seen in the foreground. Note the industrial back drop.

ANNAN ROAD TRACK PLAN

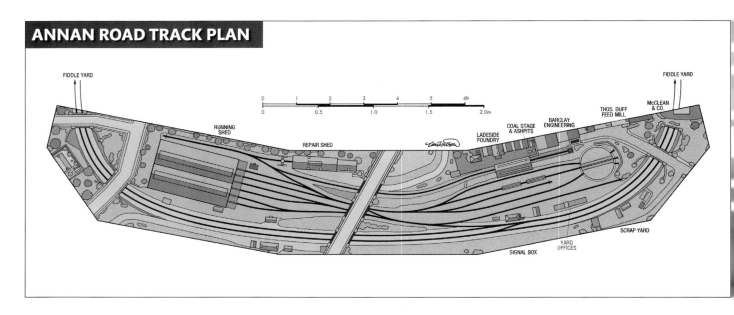

To create the space required to allow us to do this we reluctantly decided to retire and sell our much-loved Crawford Bridge layout (see February/March 2000 *BRM*), making sure that a good home was found for it. Plans were then drawn up for the storage loops and the decision made to converge the double track main lines to single track just 'off scene' and have the loops fan out from the single track allowing trains to run on either the Up or Down lines.

The usual materials have been used - 2" x 1" framing topped with 9mm thick plywood, all joints being glued and screwed. The framework supporting the storage loops is made from 1" x 1" timber onto which are fixed flush-mount brackets and the whole lot simply slots together – another new method for us which seems to work well.

Ongoing discussions during the progress of the layout dictated that where possible new methods should be tried out during the scenic construction. The Noch 'Grassmaster' was used for the first time and proved to be very successful as did the introduction of Metcalfe paving stones.

Most of the buildings have been scratch-built by various club members, each using the materials of their preferred choice. The industrial buildings adjacent to the coaling stage were inherited from Mike Bisset's Garrochburn layout. The shed has been fitted with smoke generators which add a great deal

The breakdown train waits in the siding for its next call out.

A fine study of Stanier's masterpiece. 'Duchess' Class No.46237 *City of Bristol* is coaled prior to going on shed.

of atmosphere and realism to the layout when activated.

Stock and operation

There is a wide variety of motive power available from members' collections. Ex-LMS, LNER and BR Standard classes can all be seen – all suitably weathered.

As stated earlier, the fact that the storage loops fan out from a single track means that the trains are bi-directional and this reduces the number of loops required. It also means that less complicated movements are required when changing locomotives.

We usually stock the layout with two expresses, one parcels, one local passenger, three goods, the breakdown train and a coal train for the supply of locomotives on-shed.

There is no set procedure for the operation of the layout but we do tend to operate it more as a shed layout than a main line layout and this allows light engine wrong line running both from and to the shed.

The loaded coal train is usually held in the storage loops until the breakdown train is moved off shed. On arrival the train is shunted to the shed area and split into two rakes of four wagons – the train locomotive and brake van then depart to the storage loops. The wagons are then moved to the coaling stage where they are 'emptied' behind the scenes. Once it has been re-marshalled it can then be moved back on to the main line after the train locomotive and brake van arrive on shed and from there back to the storage loops.

The breakdown crane is a heavily modified and weathered Hornby 75 ton model. The jib runner has extra storage compartments above and below the deck of the wagon, a spreader bar and chains have also been added. The rigging and associated components on the original have been removed and replaced and further detailing has been added to the body of the crane.

Annan Road made its debut at Model Rail Scotland in 2010 and has been well received wherever it has attended since then. It is a layout which has changed quite a bit from the initial concept and has given our members great pleasure in operating it.

In conclusion, our thanks must go to Tony Wright for taking the time to visit our clubrooms where the excellent photographs were taken. **BRM**

A3 No.60082 *Neil Gow* is turned prior to its next turn of duty.

RTR chassis upgrade

Tony Wright shows you how to replace those erratic running chassis on older OO gauge RTR locomotives. *Photography by the author.*

The finished 2P 4-4-0 in portrait pose and in operation on the little trainset bit of Little Bytham. The new frames make a big visual improvement as well as the much better running achieved. The guard irons on the front frames are a big plus (rather than their being on the bogie) and lamp irons on the front platform add to the betterment. The loco has since been renumbered (40610 was Scottish-based) and the capuchon removed from the chimney.

In many respects, this account is potentially rather out of date, as most of the locomotive types featured now have super-smooth, loco-powered chassis, rendering alteration to something better rather superfluous, unless one is converting to the more accurate 4mm standard gauges. However, the split chassis or tender-drive dinosaurs are still out there in their legions, driven to oblivion by better technology and confined to sidings, boxes, second-hand stalls or eBay.

The last-mentioned alternatives might render rich pickings at bargain-basement prices, just waiting for someone to acquire those dud runners and stick a decent chassis underneath them. This is the main reason for offering these notes, in the hope that it might inspire others to try these techniques themselves. I know 'inspire' sounds a bit high-handed on my part, but more and more I hear of fewer modellers being prepared to actually 'do' things for themselves.

Ready-to-run excellence
One can't deny the excellence of what's available now ready-to-run and not just in OO gauge. But in conversation recently with some kit manufacturers, sales appear to be heavily dented whenever a new RTR equivalent offering appears. If we're not careful, skills will diminish and the hobby will be the poorer, especially if some kit manufacturers give up.

Right now, the products needed to upgrade are still out there, so my advice, even if you're not contemplating an immediate re-chassis

programme, is to acquire what you need as soon as possible. And, being contentious as usual, haven't you noticed a 'sameness' about many mainstream OO (main line) layouts recently in the model press, especially with regard to motive power and rolling stock?

The chassis conversion 'guinea pigs' on these pages comprise a pair of Airfix 4Fs, a Hornby tender-drive 2P, and a Mainline/Palitoy N2. A little further on in the *Annual* a Hornby tender-drive 'Dean Goods', a Bachmann split-chassis B1 and the same firm's V2 get the same treatment. With one exception, all were horrific runners – noisy, jerky, impossible to get to run through 'scale' points (the under-scale back-to-backs made them 'bump' through turnouts and crossings), and definitely not fit for purpose.

It was the original intention to make a DVD of the processes, and part of this was shot, only to be subsequently binned. A pity, because done properly, it might well have proved successful. Never mind, I still have the stills, and I hope these prove of some use to other modellers. As usual, because any possible upgrades representing locos from the East/Midlands were of no use to me, the Southern does not feature. My apologies, though the techniques described are equally applicable to, say, a Bachmann 'Lord Nelson' or early Hornby 'Schools'. As for the 'Dean Goods'? Obviously, they were extremely uncommon on the ECML, but this model was done specifically for Simon Kohler of Hornby as a goodwill gesture to show him what was possible. Perhaps a loco-drive

'Dean Goods' will eventually appear, but for now decent running can only be achieved by building a replacement chassis.

Despite a hefty increase in price with regard to the 'proper'-chassisied locos we have now, don't expect these 'solutions' to the problems of poor running to be cheaper than buying what's now available. Even though the earlier duds might be picked up relatively cheaply, there is a high cost consequence in what I'm about to show as an alternative to jerky performance. Etched chassis are not cheap, neither are decent, high-quality can motors, and the current Markits wheelsets are very high-value indeed. No, these guinea pigs will end up being more expensive than the newcomers.

I made that!
One might ask, why bother? You'll see that two of the loco types featured are still only available with hopeless drives, so if you want good running, what's to be described is the only solution in my view. Secondly, when this piece was started two years ago, decent chassis on the guinea pig locos weren't even on the radar. Finally, at least the notion of actually building loco chassis might encourage some modellers to have a go themselves, and even contemplate full loco kit-building. Yes, we can all enjoy and exploit the better standards now on offer but, I assure you, nothing can give greater pleasure, in my opinion, than watching a locomotive run round a layout, particularly at an exhibition, and be able to say 'I made that'.

THE 4FS

hat better than prototype inspiration? Here's 44422
the Nene Valley Railway in the summer of 2010 -
ft-hand drive, no splasher beading and Stanier
imney. It even has coal rails on the tender, should you
sh to use those from SEF in modelling this loco.

One of the hideous originals and one of the replacement chassis. The replacement frames (loco and tender) are from South Eastern Finecast, wheels from Markits and motor/gearbox from DJH. Though principally designed for its own 4F kit, the frames are perfectly suited (with a little modification) for fitting underneath an Airfix 4F.

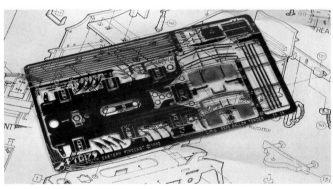

The fret for SEF's tender frames, including various tender parts, including coal rails – an added bonus. You'll note in the centre of the fret, and on the drawing, a kind of lug arrangement for fixing the rear end of the frames into slots in the cast tender body of SEF's 4F. These must be removed for fixing to the Airfix tender body.

ough perfectly sweet-running, the DJH gearbox does require some surgery to the
nderneath of the boiler and is visible once installed. For the second 4F, I substituted
ne of Comet's extremely simple gear mounts, under-slinging it so that it wasn't visible
nderneath the body. If possible, I prefer to drive on the centre axle of a six-coupled
assis - the simpler Comet mount is probably the preferable solution, though it doesn't
n quite as sweetly. Note how the turned spacers have been soldered in place, fixed to
atch the original fixing positions of the Airfix body. For attachment to a SEF 4F body,
ne would merely screw them in using the appropriate holes. This isn't a problem, as all
e various chassis have been jig-assembled, either using Comet's own or my ancient
mieson original.

As received, the Airfix 4F body has a slug of lead running right through it. This must be removed by unscrewing it and then taking off the smokebox front to let it drop out. Cut in half, the front bit can then be used again, leaving space in the firebox for a replacement motor. To balance the ballast, I've added 'Liquid Lead' around the rear fixing pillar.

oth 4Fs finished and up and running on their new
ts of frames. The 4F body has left-hand drive and
splasher beading, meaning an LMS-built
ample, so take care when re-numbering. 44519
as a Stanier chimney (from SEF) for variation, and
eathering completes the job.

THE 2P

I had two 2Ps to fiddle with, though only re-chassied the BR one. This was the one left alone, and very pretty don't you think? It's a pity the tender-drive was so hit and miss as a system, otherwise it might have proved popular.

The original chassis (top) and what I fitted underneath as a replacement. Everything here (frame-wise) is courtesy of Comet, including their gearbox. The motor's an appropriate Mashima and all the wheels are from Markits. The loco chassis is a perfect fit, designed for the loco body and needs only dressing of etching cusps for it to fit snugly.

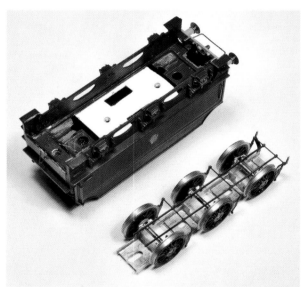

Though the tender chassis is right for a 2P, fitting it to the established tender body requires some ingenuity. Here I've taken out a considerable amount of plastic from underneath to give clearances (dental burr in a mini drill) and to fix the two together I've made a 'plate' of thickish plastic card', solvent-fixed to the frames. Two superglued-on 8BA nuts give the fixing points and, providing not too much screwing-up pressure is applied, the two hold together perfectly.

Hornby's current 2P now has this superb loco-drive mechanism, complete with can motor and flywheel. All wheels are much finer (though I still remain sceptical about traction tyres) and any thoughts of completely replacing this would be daft. However, note that I've already simplified the wiring by connecting the leads from the loco pick-ups directly to the motor tags, dispensing with the tender pick-up wires. This chassis has pick-ups on the bogie as well as the drivers and on decent track with live-frog points doesn't need tender pick-ups.

There are still things to be done, however, not least sorting out the huge gap between the loco and tender (and the mass of wires connecting the pair). Like most of Hornby's recent tender locos, the loco to tender connection is semi-permanent because of tender pick-ups, the socket for a decoder being inside the tender body. Discarding all these impedements, and that massive drawbar, I substituted a 'goalpost' on the loco dragbeam and a simple hook on the tender.

With no need for tender pick-ups, I replaced the original tender wheels. Their back-to-backs appear to be fixed (a bit narrow) and they're not as fine as those on the loco. Substitute Jackson/Romfords just dropped in. I also took off the original coupling fixing and substituted my standard 'Sprat & Winkle'-height 'goalpost'.

Continuing fiddling with this loco resulted in my fitting of a scale shackle to the front bufferbeam, making front footplate lamp brackets (etched brass scrap), removing the chimney's capuchon and taking off the mould line from the smokebox/boiler/firebox top. I also renumbered it to a more appropriate Nottingham-based 2P.

The difference between the different loco/tender drawgear is shown here. Why Hornby feel the need for such a huge gap is beyond me, for my substitute will go round 24" curves with ease. Perhaps it's because of all the wires – tender pick-ups and DCC necessities? I have no need of the former and don't want the latter. By the way, the replaced two last figures in the BR loco's number do rather show up - weathering will disguise this.

The Hornby/Airfix 'Dean Goods', and Bachmann's (ex-Mainline) B1 and V2 get the Tony Wright treatment as he continues his locomotive upgrades on page 36.

40632 (now slightly weathered and with crew installed) in operation on Little Bytham, crossing Ian Wilson's soon-to-be-installed bridge over Station Road.

THE N2

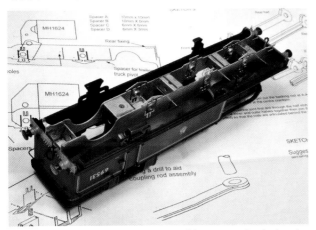

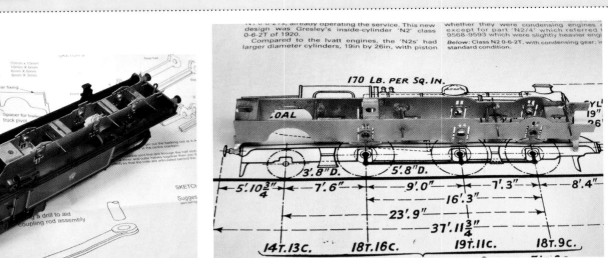

As far as I know, as yet, the Hornby N2 doesn't have a new chassis, though one might well be in the pipeline. Obviously, this old one can't have tender drive and it doesn't have a split chassis, but its running was still abysmal. So, a substitute set of Comet frames was ordered and made up. So far so good.

Though designed for the Airfix N2, something appears to have gone wrong with Comet's measurements. When placed against a scale drawing, with the rear axle lined up, the other axles don't match.

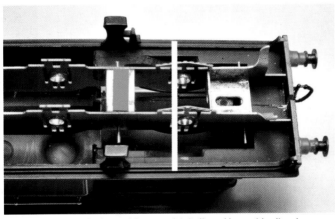

The front axle is too far forward, how much is indicated here with a line drawn through the centre of the splashers.

In fact, it turns out all the wheel centres are too far forward. The solution is to remove the rear guard irons and file the 'L'-shaped slots further back until the frames are in the right position. Then re-solder the guard irons back on.

The protruding lengths of the frames have been cut off and the rear spacer moved back, necessitating some cutting away of its vertical face to clear the pony wheels. The buffers have also gone, of which more later.

The front drivers now match up with the splashers (perhaps the body is 'out', not the chassis), though the frames no longer touch the rear of the bufferbeam. Still, when all the added pipework is in place, the discrepancy is invisible.

My chosen prototype, 69521, had extra handrails on the tanksides and retained its GNR buffers. As far as I know, the firm MPD no longer trades (I have an extensive spares box), though GNR sprung buffers can be sourced from Alan Gibson or Markits.

ffers added and the loco renumbered. It's parked on ne prototype source material, courtesy of Keith Pirt and lin Walker. Always refer to decent prototype pictures en model making.

Replacement and original chassis side by side. A DJH gearbox and Mashima motor supply the super smooth performance. I've added all the extra pipework around the bufferbeams as part of the chassis because solder gives a much better bond than glue. The original chassis's motor was very powerful but the performance was rubbish with regard to quiet and smooth running.

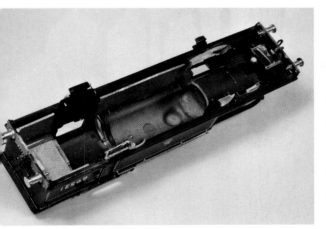

e huge weight in the original chassis at least gave plenty of weight for nesion. With this gone, lead strip was glued inside the body to give adequate last as a substitute.

Fresh from overhaul at 'The Plant', the now sweet-running N2 scoots through Little Bytham light engine (where's the shedplate?). On every featured model all the new front numberplates came from Ian Wilson's Pacific Models range.

On a different occasion, the loco heads south from Doncaster this time bunker-first. Note the correctly-positioned tail lamp.

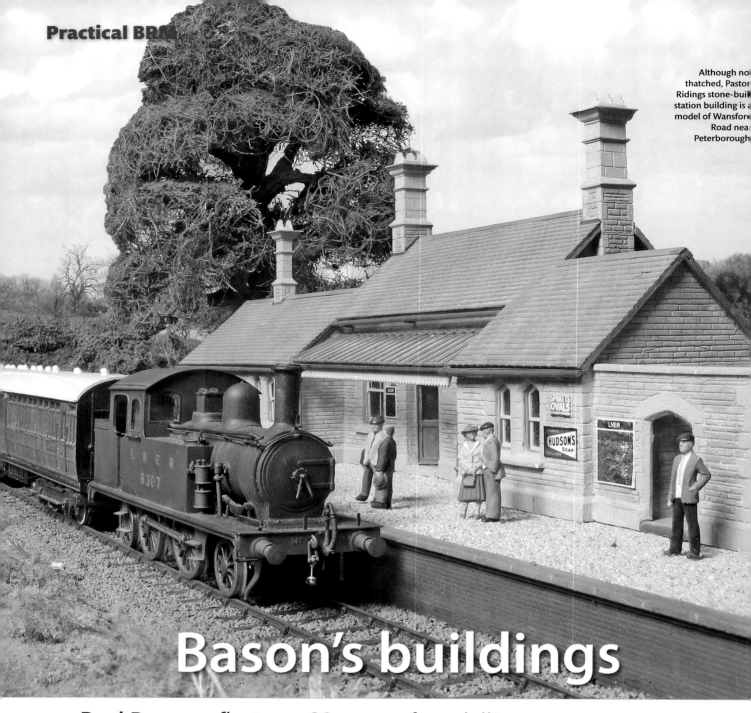

Although not thatched, Paston Ridings stone-built station building is a model of Wansford Road near Peterborough

Bason's buildings

Paul Bason reflects on 20 years of modelling. *Photography by the author.*

Doesn't time fly when you're having fun? It really doesn't seem like 20 years since I was putting together my very first feature for the brand new *British Railway Modelling* magazine. Who would have thought then that some 86 features, 82 reviews and a staggering 2,662 photos later, that I would still be writing features for the magazine and would be photographing layouts too? Ok, so you might think that I am sad keeping a tally that I have contributed to 658 pages (including photographs) but I am, after all, a Chartered Quantity Surveyor and from that comes more than just a passing interest in building construction.

It all started when, having already had a few small features and photos in the now defunct *Model Railways* magazine (who covered my medal winning cottages at the Model Engineer Exhibition a few years earlier)

I was approached by *BRM's* first editor David Brown to write a piece for the new mag. Luckily my other main hobby has always been photography and, although I hadn't deliberately taken stage by stage photos, I had taken enough fairly presentable ones to illustrate the article without too much trouble. David let me have a peek at the mock up magazine and, following a chat with him about the new format, was pleasantly surprised to learn that the man behind the exciting new venture was Michael Warner who I knew from my days working in John Fowler's model shop in Peterborough on Saturdays some years earlier. Indeed I had got a shoebox full of his GWR kit-built locos running for him and had built a Will's 61xx as a sort of commission while I was still at school.

My input to that first *BRM* was a five-page feature introducing the scratch-building skills needed to construct the thatched cottages for

Paston Ridings, my EM gauge LNER layout that was still very much under construction at the time. The article summarised basic building construction in plastic card but tactfully left out thatching which was held back by the Editor until issue No.2. Reading the feature 20 years on it is pleasing to see that my ethos (if I may use a posh word) was the same then as it is now. Essentially I only started scratch-building model cottages because I wanted to prove that you don't have to be a super qualified modeller with years of experience to knock up something reasonably presentable in a fairly short period of time. I had read an article in an old magazine back in 1982 and, really wanting to have a go at thatching for myself, measured up and photographed a local pub (well why not!). The resulting 'Green Man' may be a bit rough around the edges, and may not be quite up to my current standards, but it still looks like a well-weathered thatch and did just what

I was hoping; it proved that thatching is not as hard as some folks make out and certainly gave me the confidence to make a whole village full of cottages that still sit proudly on the end of my layout.

Although some readers might think that those who write articles like this must be really prolific model makers, I certainly am not. Like most people, work, the family, other hobbies all have a call on my time. Indeed, after the initial push with the first half a dozen cottages, the layout took up a lot of my modelling time so new cottage construction was pretty much intermittent to say the least. Admittedly my collection, as you can see from the accompanying photos, has been added to from time to time but, having scratch-built my first loco when I was 14, I couldn't just make buildings on their own and nothing else.

Despite the passage of time, my basic method remains pretty much the same although I now use solvent-free contact adhesive to fix the thatch. Essentially the

Where it all started - the first three cottages that I made almost 30 years ago.

Visitors to the National Festival of Railway Modelling at Peterborough may have driven by nearby Alwalton Post Office - here it is in model form.

Duck Street Cottage has a family connection - being my Mum's birthplace it had to be the subject of my most recent cottage!

building comprises a shell made up from components all made from two sheets of 40 thou. plastic card laminated together. Not only does this make the resulting structure nice and rigid but also prevents warping and distortion over time. Where the walls represent stonework, each stone is scribed onto the face of the plastic by hand using a scraper board tool. Thatching is plumber's hemp trimmed to shape using a pair of curved nail scissors.

My structure modelling in the last 20 years hasn't all been thatched. I spent an enjoyable couple of years making a host of buildings that enabled the late Michael Warner to finish his Moreton-In-Marsh to Shipston-on-Stour layout. Although I cannot admit to being a fan of the Great Western I do miss my Saturday morning visits to see Michael and his wife Jean as the small collection of models progressed. Regular readers might recall these as they were featured as an occasional series in the mag.

Having somehow won the scratch-building competition with various buildings off the EM layout at the King's Lynn O Gauge Group's Christmas Dinner for several years, the likes of Bob Pearman and John Hobden have often asked when am I going to move on to bigger (and better?) things and build a cottage in 7mm scale? Well Bob and John, I have started one and what a size it is particularly when you have been a 4mm fan for years. With work progressing slowly I am keeping my new project under wraps for the time being, but as soon as it is finished - whenever that might be! - I am sure that the editor will find space to include it in *BRM*.

With other projects such as my O gauge live steam loco and the complete remodelling of my 1980-built narrow gauge layout in hand; work over the last 20 years on Paston Ridings has been a 'now and again' sort of thing. It has been to a handful of shows since *BRM* began but, as it is far too large to put up in its entirety at home, has spent much of its time boxed up and in storage. With a few new cottages to put into the scene, and for that matter a couple half-planned, I might just get it out and give it a makeover. Who knows I might even add on another couple of baseboards!

Royal Oak cottage was featured on the very first cover of *BRM* - in fact it is a model of a pub in the village of Castor but given a garden setting.

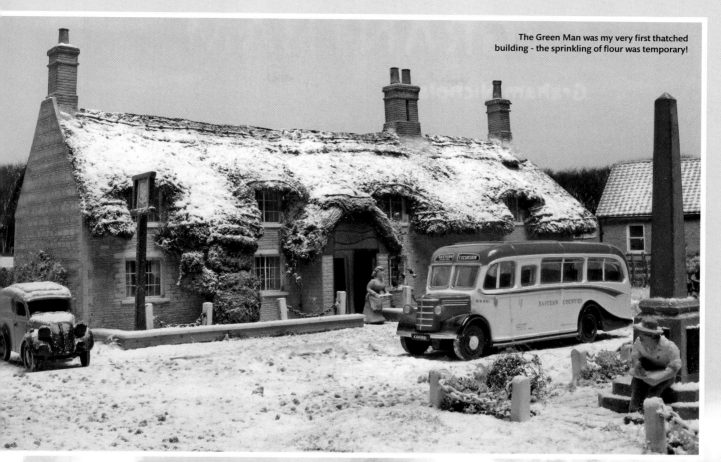

The Green Man was my very first thatched building - the sprinkling of flour was temporary!

The Bluebell Inn and the cottages either side are based on historical photos of the Dogsthorpe area of Peterborough.

GRANTHAM

Graham Nicholas outlines his future layout plans
for this 4mm scale project. *Photography by Tony Wright*

The leather strap on the old compartment door window has been practically worn out during the seemingly interminable journey across from the East Midlands. But at last, with the young lad's head poking out of the window once more, they finally swing alongside the gleaming rails of the East Coast Main Line and approach journey's end. As they do so, A1 No.2558 *Tracery* strides past, heading north with a long rake of immaculately varnished teak coaches. 'There you are lad, what about that?' says Grandad.

Setting foot on the platform, the little boy can hardly contain his excitement. There is activity everywhere. A southbound express swings into the station, coming smartly to a stand. In no time at all, the train engine is

detached and the fresh engine moves out from beside the signalbox to take its place. A hurried guard's whistle and the express is on its way again, the rhythmical sound of the engine's exhaust fading into a dull roar as it builds up momentum for the climb ahead of it. Meanwhile, the relieved engine has already backed through the station and is away to the engine sheds alongside the station.

In that direction, a general haze clouds the activity, but various apple green apparitions can be glimpsed. Pilot locos fuss about with odd horse boxes and merchandise vans. A constant stream of freight trains slip through the station area almost unnoticed.

Finally, the sight they've come to see. The bells ring and the signals clatter once again. An unusual hush descends upon the station. Then away in the southern distance comes a strange new sound. A cross between a shriek and a

wail heralds the impending approach of an express train like no other. It is clearly moving at speed yet viewed down the long straight approaching the station it's appearance takes a few agonising moments more as the excitement mounts to a crescendo.

Suddenly with a final urgent warning blast on the whistle it bursts from under the footbridge and is upon them, flashing past their noses in a blur of blue and stainless steel. As it recedes rapidly away round the sweeping curve to the north, the legend on the end of the elegantly shaped rear coach proclaims 'The Coronation'. The little lad missed the loco name but old hand Grandad saw it sure enough. 4488 *Union of South Africa*, specially built for the new service and still only a few months old.

This then is Grantham 1937. A world seemingly full of endless thrills and excitement for the young trainspotter. But on their way back home, Grandad reflects on some of the anomalies. If the LNER can build such a truly impressive modern express train, capable of whisking its passengers from English to

General view of the station with a northbound express slowing for its stop. Most of the buildings are just card mock ups at this stage with the exception of the main station buildings which have been assembled (by Mrs Nicholas!) and just await chimneys and guttering. The photo-shopped area behind the coal train is where the MPD will be.

South Box junction, the least developed part of the layout so far. The pointwork at bottom left is where northbound trains have a choice of three routes - Down Main, Down Passenger Relief, or Down Goods Relief - controlled by a magnificent three-way bracket somersault signal (to be installed in due course). The coal train is making its way out of the lay-by (recess) siding provided at this point - there must have been some congestion in the station area!

Scottish capitals in a mere six hours, what is this ancient six-wheel coach they're sat in, with its bone-jarring ride quality and 19th century locomotive wheezing away at the front – the very antithesis of the streamliner they've just been to see? And he'd also clocked the greatly increased coal (going south) and iron ore traffic (heading north) passing through the station?

The harsh truth is that, in 1937, Britain is a country reeling from the long years of depression and the LNER is feeling it as keenly as anyone. More significantly, the coal is for the naval fleets massing at the southern ports and the iron ore is feeding the

hungry blast furnaces of Humberside, military preparations belatedly driving up the demand for steel. Although they didn't know it at the time, within two years the country would be at war and the iconic streamliners would be mothballed, never to return, in a world changed forever.

So why Grantham?

The concept of Grantham came about as the fusion of three different thought streams. It's by no means a logical end result for a BR Midland Region 1950s modeller! But others were to influence the decision and I have to say that, once immersed in the concept, I have been utterly captivated.

The story starts with 'Thomas'. Pardon?! Well, yes it is partly true. Grantham's

predecessor as an exhibition layout was a 10' x 5' main line 'Thomas' layout that made a few brief appearances between 2004 and 2007. Built for my son Thomas (pure coincidence!), without any prompting, Nicholas junior developed a penchant for things apple green, teak and streamlined. When considering a subject for the next project – and having rather outgrown the world of Sodor(!) – a 1930s LNER subject was therefore the natural starting point. Mentally travelling north along the ECML, it took about 30 seconds to arrive at Grantham.

Ah Grantham! Now there's a place to conjure with. Express trains, loco changes, a depot (allowing a decent selection of locos on view), yet surprisingly compact (compared to other 'classic' East Coast railway centres like York or Newcastle). Yes, there was definitely potential in this idea.

Meanwhile, I do have some personal association with Grantham – enter thought stream two. My mother's side of the family

At the south end of the main Up (to London) platform was situated 'Yard' box, attended by the distinctive co-acting junction signal (the lower, right-hand signal arms control access to the Up goods relief line which commenced at this point). Work is underway on the platforms following due research. Their height was surprisingly low (photos show platform top was below bottom of loco buffer beam); also their surfaces were largely of flags pre-war, which gives a more pleasing appearance than the plain asphalt coverings that gradually replaced them in BR days.

hails from Lincolnshire and every summer there would be the annual pilgrimage to Boston, Wainfleet and Skegness. This was the 1970s and the principal leg of our journey was the 'Harwich Boat Train' from Manchester. Having wandered across the Peak District (*via* the Hope Valley) the inevitable Class 37 picked its way *via* Chesterfield and Nottingham to deposit us at Grantham, where the 'first generation' DMU would be ticking over patiently in the bay to take us on the final leg across the flat Fenlands.

Somehow, Grantham 'struck a chord' even then. Maybe it was indeed that after the long, weary drag across the country, suddenly here was a main line railway. The blue 'boxes on wheels' never did much for me but I at least recognised a distinctive junction station

of some character.

My father too also talks of the Grantham of yore. He, at least, experienced the place in the days of steam, making a similar journey to me some 20 years previously on account of his National Service in Lincolnshire (hence the family 'connection'). Colin Walker's *Trails through Grantham* was a favourite book to pore over

together on a rainy Sunday lunchtime.

But it was when I mooted the idea to some friends that the third element of the story came together. I got an excited response from fellow Trustee and Chairman of the A1 Steam Locomotive Trust – Mark Allatt. 'I've thought about doing Grantham and have a large stock of 1930s LNER rolling stock', enthused the e-mail. Strangely, I hadn't given much thought as to stock up to this point but it was obvious that a large fleet would be needed to do the model justice. And here apparently was a ready-made answer to a large part of that conundrum.

A very pleasant evening in Mark's company some months later, pouring over his collection of ready-to-run and kit-built stock, 'sealed the deal'. Mark's own leaning to all things LNER (as befits his A1 Chairman status) was manifest in his collection of models. Here was a 1930s LNER fleet with nowhere to run – so I would build the layout and he would provide the stock. Grantham was 'on'!

Transition to model

So what exactly would we attempt to model? In reality, Grantham in the 1930s would have been a world full of contrasts. To portray it as a constant stream of

The tracks over Harlaxton Road bridge (laid out exactly as per the original). This curve has been planned on a generous (for a model) 6' radius and naturally turns the layout towards the fiddle yard area. The choice of radius allows good use to be made of Peco curved points, which nicely match the required geometry. The approaching Up train is on the East Coast main Line, the lines diverging to the left are for Nottingham.

A view of the north end curve in its wider setting as it crosses the Harlaxton Road bridge. This is intended as a prime exhibition viewpoint from which to watch the north end action. Just ahead of the loco lie two Peco single slips arranged as a trailing crossover on a curve (as per the prototype pre-war). An explanation of my method for installing these points in this manner will, with the editor's blessing, be provided in a future article.

Gresley Pacifics at the head of gleaming express trains would be a disproportionate view of history. In the cold light of day times were tough. The streamliners were, in pure economic terms, barely more than a distraction (although great publicity) and were all the impoverished LNER could afford in the teeth of the 1930's depression. Hence the lesser services were dominated by the old GNR stock that should have been pensioned off years previously. Converting some of the six-wheelers to run as articulated bogie stock was the best of a bad job for provincial suburban services. In all truth, Grantham was probably too far away from the more politically-sensitive London commuter belt to warrant anything more.

This then is the intended ethos of the Grantham model. Sure, Gresley Pacifics and the streamlined trains will feature – but in moderation. Their counterpoint will be the ancient local services, shuffling in and out of the station, providing much gainful employment for the ousted Atlantics and their older 4-4-0 predecessors.

The loco changes will be a strong feature of the model and its operation, virtually its signature. In contrast to other 'classic' loco change locations (Crewe, Carlisle, York, Newcastle), Grantham was a relatively small and compact place. This of course makes it relatively model-able whilst retaining operational interest. With automatic couplers (Kadees), a loco change is relatively easy to do and gives a *modus operandi* for the depot (as per the prototype).

Grantham was also quite a junction in its heyday and a surprising number of local services started and terminated at the station. These days, when the solitary East Midlands 153 unit pauses before continuing its interminable journey to Skegness it can be easily forgotten that in times past local services headed north from Grantham towards Lincoln (via the now closed direct route from Honington) and Boston, as well as Nottingham. Some of the

My favourite from Tony's first 'shoot'. Although everything is yet a bit basic and unweathered, the eye level view gives a glimpse of the atmosphere that the layout is seeking to create. The K3 has got the Nottingham road as *Flying Fox* bears down on the station with a southbound express. In the bay platform, an elderly Atlantic waits for the fuss to die down.

The view from the steps of the North signalbox showing almost the entire station layout. To the left are the now lost Up bay platforms (permanent trackwork yet to be installed). On the main line, ex-works B17 2864 *Liverpool* has the road (probably returning to Doncaster on the popular afternoon running-in turn), while, an Atlantic waits with a Lincoln service. Next is the engine change siding, followed by the Down relief platform, where the ever-present C12 station pilot has paused in its labours. To the right is the Up and Down through goods running line, with the entrance pointwork to the loco depot on the far right. Much work remains to complete this scene but already the atmosphere of the working railway is there.

Nottingham services extended further to Derby (Friargate) and, *via* running powers retained from GNR days, to Burton-on-Trent and even Stafford (if you please!). A further service turned south off the Nottingham route at Bottesford and headed along the former GN&LNWR joint line to Leicester (Belgrave Road). Additionally, some local East Coast Main Line 'all stations' services terminated at Grantham (one in particular was a popular running in turn from Doncaster – further excuse for locomotive diversification!).

As befits a true public service that the railway used to supply so splendidly, everything was planned to connect There are pictures of a Northbound express pausing in the station, with a D2 waiting on a Lincoln train in the bay and an Atlantic waiting in the Down relief platform with the Nottingham service – simple cross platform changes. Now built-upon and barely discernible were the north end bays on the up side. It was here that the arrivals from Lincoln would terminate – and so provide another simple cross platform change for a following southbound express to London. There was also a loading bay for horseboxes, etc, in this area too. All in all, plenty to go at for an operational model railway.

What about the goods workings? Much of the longer distance traffic simply trundled through, although in both directions there were relief lines – and they still exist, albeit in slightly modified form. In the south-bound direction the Up goods relief line started immediately south of the station platform. Northbound the relief line started once the Great North road had been cleared (by South box) and threaded its way between the west side of the station and the depot. From this line, northbound goods trains could gain access to both Nottingham and East Coast Main Lines. It was actually bi-directional so that southbound trains from Nottingham could also use it. All this creates some interesting routes through the station area.

The specific case of the famous iron ore trains that ran in the area is particularly interesting. Some of these were resourced by Grantham shed and a typical cycle of operation was thus: a fresh engine from the shed would relieve a north-bound (loaded) train on the Down relief line. Upon returning several hours later with a rake of empties (from Frodingham), the train would pass straight through the station, gaining the Up relief south of the station. After a pause for water (and most likely a crew change), it would continue to Highdyke. It would then return from there with a further loaded train – but interestingly tender-first as there were no turning facilities at the Highdyke reception sidings or along the branch. So, part of the purpose of the loco being relieved at Grantham was for it to be turned.

So, a combination of loco changes, passenger services departing and terminating, horse boxes being attached/detached and goods trains being re-loco'd are all to be replicated and require 'designing in' to the model to enable this to happen. Such a variety of moves will avoid the monotony of a repetitive cavalcade through the station and allow a portrayal more closer to how it really was.

Wow – that is some design brief! **BRM**

The running lines south of the station. From bottom left to top right: Goods Reception; Up Goods Relief; Up Main; Down Main; Down Passenger Relief; Carriage Sidings; Up and Down Goods Relief; Goods Loop. The first of the 'rotating head' ground signals have been installed and are working. The K3 has charge of two Ian Kirk 'twins', my first stock contributions to the project. Together they make a 'classic' LNER four-coach suburban formation: Brake Third/Full Third + Composite (Lavatory)/Brake Third - no corridors and only one coach with a toilet!

RTR chassis upgrade

More RTR locos get the **Tony Wright** treatment! *Photography by the author.*

Because these ready-to-run chassis upgrades were originally intended to be shown on a DVD, these are not a blow-by-blow series of accounts. That said, my methods of making loco frames are probably well known by now through hundreds of articles, and books and DVDs. Anyway, if you wish to see the locos 'live' as it were, there's a sequence available on the *BRM* website right now.

Finally, just as an afterthought, and revealing my natural hypocrisy yet again, I've added a little something with regard to the 2P 4-4-0 and B1 4-6-0, where Hornby's and Bachmann's latest super runners have been 'tweaked' just a bit to make them a little better and a bit more personal - I'll let the pictures tell the stories.

THE B1

All the bits needed from Comet for a full replacement B1 set of frames and motive power.

With a set of Markits proper wheels this is what you should finish up with.

Above: But first you have to examine why a replacement chassis is required. The furthest chassis is the replacement just getting underway. The two nearer ones are a couple of manifestations of the original Bachmann (ex-Palitoy) split chassis. Both are absolute shockers with regard to running. Press releases from Bachmann suggest that the latest (non split) chassis are supplied because of DCC imperatives (split chassis are an absolute pain to fit DCC decoders), rather than because of poor running at source - I beg to differ!

Left: I've re-chassied several Bachmann B1s now and in case you're wondering why the motor appears to be back to front in the frames underneath Umseke, then it's because it works better that way going forwards. No matter how carefully one erects Comet, Markits or DJH gearboxes, they're always quieter going one way than the other, and it's inconsistent as to which. The other B1 in this shot has its 'box more conventionally mounted, because it runs better that way going forwards, and it's forward-going best performance that we're after. Note the added 'Liquid Lead' and lead ballast, obviously differently positioned dependent on the aspect of the gearbox. Naturally, this renders an incompatibility between the pair, and you can't just swop chassis around.

And this is what the replacement chassis looks like underneath the original Bachmann body. Original, in that it's from Bachmann, though I've renumbered and renamed it, added a proper front shackle, close coupled the loco and tender, added real coal and applied some weathering.

I've mentioned several B1 chassis jobs undertaken before, and here we have an earlier Comet B1 chassis (front) alongside a later one. The drives are different I know but the earlier chassis displays Comet's mistake in using the Roche drawing as a guide. Because of this, the position of the die block and the expansion link are pivoted too far back in the radius rod, thus making the eccentric rod too short, upsetting the whole geometry of the thing.

in service on Little Bytham.

Yet another Bachmann B1 undergoing a chassis rebuild. 61159 was the B1 that worked the 'Leicester' for a time over the M&GNR during the line's final year, so this one will run on Bytham's little railway. Note the frames held accurately in the jig and parts of the springs removed to accommodate pick-ups.

And now for an extra bit regarding B1s. I mentioned in my review of Hornby's B1 how I was disappointed with the shape of the chimney. So, off it came and a replacement from Markits glued on in its place.

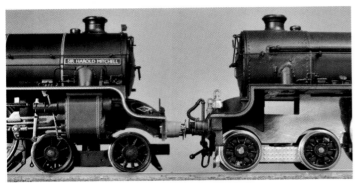

In fairness to Hornby, the chimney they fit is no worse than the firm's competitors, and perhaps I'll need to undertake a few replacements on my Bachmann locos in due course.

I believe you can tell the difference and, in my opinion, the replacement (right) is superior. What can't be argued with is how much better the replacement Markits bogie wheels look.

Above: Renumbered and detailed, Hornby's B1 fits in perfectly as it performs pick-up duties on Little Bytham. One would be mad to contemplate a new chassis for this model, unless one were changing gauge.

Right: That same madness would be needed to re-chassis this latest Bachmann B1. All I've done is replace the bogie wheels, change its identity, close couple loco and tender, install a crew, add real coal and apply some more weathering. It's performance is superb and it performs pick-up duties (for which faultless, slow-speed running in both directions is essential) with admirable ease.

HE V2

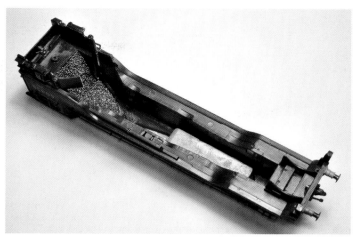

Extra ballast is always necessary when fitting replacement etched-brass chassis and how much has been added can be observed here – flat lead and 'Liquid Lead'. Note also the previously-modified outside rear frames.

...sual view of the old and new. At least this original chassis ran reasonably well, if ...e on the wobbly side. As can be seen, I'd already altered the hideous Cartazzi ... The Comet replacement is up and running.

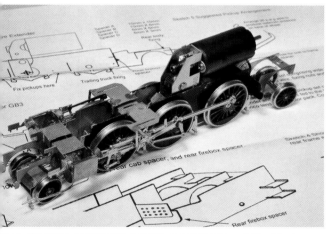

Complete and weathered - I've also addressed the problem of the puny dome by fitting a cast replacement from DMR. The issues regarding the other 'problems' with Bachmann's V2 body still remain – the filled-in look to the bottom of the boiler and the 'flat' look to what should be a rearward slope to the top of the firebox. However, on a layout this loco looks entirely presentable, though I do think Bachmann has missed a trick in not upgrading the V2 body to the same standard as the wonderful new chassis.

...hock of the new', and this Comet chassis really makes up well. The drive is ...ly apposite for a V2 – a big, fat Mashima can motor driving through a multi- ... Markits gearbox. Fast, powerful, quiet, silky-smooth and beautifully free- ...ng. What more could one ask for? Funnily enough, it's just the same as ...mann's replacement V2 chassis, recently introduced. Note the cylinder drain ... joggled out to give clearance for the pony wheels. Not quite prototypical but ...st they're there full-length.

In service on Little Bytham.

THE 'DEAN GOODS'

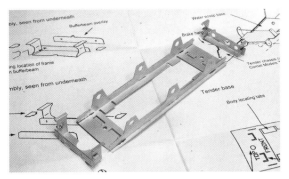

>These are Comet's outside frames for the Dean tender - I didn't bother mucking about with the plastic originals (too much work already undertaken with regard to the 2P and the 4Fs).

Once more comparisons between the two. As with the second 4F, I used an under-slung arrangement of Comet's simplest gear mount, this time with a very small Mashima motor.

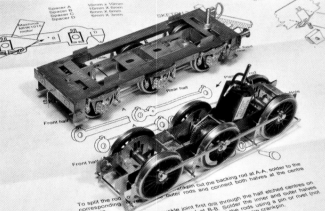

As with the 4F, the slug of lead had to be removed, this time by temporarily taking off the cab. 'Liquid Lead' was fixed in as many places as possible (using superglue), including the underneath of the tender coalspace.

The complete replacement tender frameset, though requiring having to be made, was a much easier job than that on the 2P and 4Fs. The loco chassis is a very neat piece of etching.

Isn't this much, much nicer, visually and mechanically, especially after painting? Further jobs I should have done were the making and fixing of lampirons, fitting proper numberplates and adding real coal. Simon Kohler could do that if he wished!

PROTOTYPE INSPIRATION

-hand prototype reference is essential for success, especially with regard to valve gear detail. Here's just such a set of pictures of B1 motion, taken at Barrow Hill in 2010.

WEATHERED MOTION

ugh showing preserved (and thus clean) locos' motion, it's never shiny as illustrated by these shots showing respectively a 'Battle of Britain', Standard 5MT and 'King ur'. Never leave etched nickel silver rods and gear in its shiny state, even if the loco's just ex-works.

Third rail and semaphores

Graeme Elgar travels around the South Eastern Division and samples last day services with the 2-EPBs. *Photography by the author.*

Blue 5753 arriving at Selsdon bound for Elmers End on May 13, 1983.

May 13, 1983, was just another Friday for a bored sixth former in South London. The usual round of educational tedium came and went for me as I was readily distracted by the flow of freight on the Dartford Loop Line which passed beside the school. The four o'clock bell went and it was time for me to make my way to Lee station to catch the 16.14 to Lewisham, thence down the mid-Kent to Elmers End to take in the last trains on the Sanderstead service. The line from Woodside to Selsdon was to be closed after the last train of the day, leaving Elmers End as a junction for the frequent 'popper' to Addiscombe, and meaning the closure of Bingam Road, Coombe Road and Selsdon stations. At Elmers End I changed to the first service, an Addiscombe bound 'popper' which left at Woodside and took a couple of pictures of the South Eastern Railway signal box and junction signals. The next Down train was for Sanderstead and I enjoyed a run down in 5725, freshly repainted in blue/grey livery. At Sanderstead I crossed over to the Up platform and watched 5725 head down clear of the crossover, and after much chattering from the signal box, return to pick up some passengers for Elmers End.

I got out at Selsdon, just in time for plain blue 5763 on a Down train to arrive. I hadn't realised at the time that Selsdon was the last station in the London area to still have gas lighting, and wish now that I'd taken a lot more pictures of the infrastructure, rather tham just the trains themselves. An all blue 'Thumper' unit passed towards Oxted and it wasn't long before 5763 returned with the Elmers End train which I joined. A quick couple of pics at Elmers End and it was back down to

Woodside signal box on May 13, 1983.

Sanderstead again and back up to Selsdon where, much to the driver's annoyance, I nipped out to get a picture and leapt back on again! And so back to Elmers End and Lewisham to get back to Sidcup and the joys of the 'will it or won't it come' 51 'bus home!

Decline and closure

The line had been in decline for a number of years, and was threatened with closure in the Beeching Report, but reprieved. However, through services from Sanderstead to London via Catford were withdrawn in the mid-1970s, leaving the line open for the morning and evening weekday peaks, although patronage was not that great even then with a 2-EPB being more than sufficient. From the standard of the ride, and the fact that most of the line was laid with bullhead rail, it would have been hard to justify track renewals on such a line as that.

The line was lifted the following year, leaving Elmers End to be a junction for Addiscombe only. Woodside lost its junction status (the signalbox being closed soon after), and a short stub at Selsdon was left as a headshunt for the

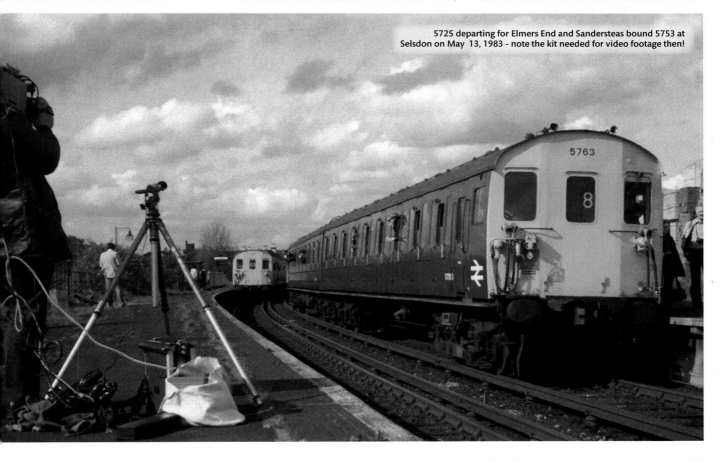

5725 departing for Elmers End and Sandersteas bound 5753 at Selsdon on May 13, 1983 - note the kit needed for video footage then!

Layout Planning

6231 at Borough Market Junction with a Cannon Street-Greenwich- Dartford service on July 3, 1985.

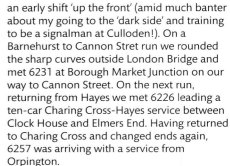

6257 arriving at Charing Cross from Orpington on July 3, 1985.

an early shift 'up the front' (amid much banter about my going to the 'dark side' and training to be a signalman at Culloden!). On a Barnehurst to Cannon Stret run we rounded the sharp curves outside London Bridge and met 6231 at Borough Market Junction on our way to Cannon Street. On the next run, returning from Hayes we met 6226 leading a ten-car Charing Cross-Hayes service between Clock House and Elmers End. Having returned to Charing Cross and changed ends again, 6257 was arriving with a service from Orpington.

On Saturday July 6, 1985, whilst waiting to go to Tonbridge and Eridge to cover another 'last day', Stores Unit 018 passed through

oil terminal there. A fresh breath came to the line in the form of the Croydon Tramlink which runs over some of the trackbed. One station, Bingham Road, had a small claim to fame when it was used for scenes in Tony Hancock's 1961 film, 'The Rebel'.

Even in the early '80s I always carried a camera with me and occasionally I would be lucky enough to be given a cab ride. This gave a whole new perspective on the complex lines around London Bridge and Charing Cross, and some results are seen here. Also, at this time the units were renumbered from their 57xx series to match their TOPS classification (Class 416/2), but only showed the last four digits on their fronts, becoming 62xx.

I started with BR in 1983, moving just about as far as possible away from third rail territory to Inverness, but frequently came back to visit friends and family. A chance meeting with a Grove Park driver during a July 1985 visit gained me an invitation to travel with him for

5763 at Elmers End on May 13, 1983 with a fine collection of cars in the car park!

Stores unit 018 passes Orpington on a Stewarts Lane-Ashford Chart Leacon working on July 6, 1985.

Blue/grey 6236 sporting the NSE 'flash' on the front at Grove Park having just arrived from Bromley North with a 'popper' in October 1990.

Orpington on a Stewarts Lane to Ashford Chart Leacon working. This unit was formed by coupling two modified DMBS (Driving Motor Brake Second) vehicles taken from ex-North Tyneside units - No.65318 (ex-5788) and 65324 (ex-5794) - and modifying them to suit their new role. The former Tyneside units were immediately identified by a smaller headcode panel and larger guard's brake area, and spent most of their Southern life on the South Western Division, occasionally straying to the South Eastern Division for attention at Slade Green depot or during shortages.

Another 2-EPB stronghold in south east London was the Grove Park to Bromley North branch which they worked during 'off-peak' times. Until the early '80s it was possible in the rush hours to travel directly between Bromley North and Charing Cross, with the units returning to Bromley North to be stabled through the day. However, economy measures at Grove Park meant that the points and crossings were removed when it came time for their renewal, leaving the only access to/from the branch through a trailing crossover from the Up Fast to the branch platform at the north end of the station. When I travelled it last in October 1990, 6236 was in charge.

Preservation
The EPG Preservation Group own 5759 which has been restored to 1960s condition at Shepherdswell on the East Kent Railway. It is currently in green livery with small yellow warning panels and is in use on certain weekends during the year, being hauled along the line by one of the resident locos. Visit their website (www.epbg.co.uk) for details.

As ever in this life, we look back and wish for certain things. Mine are digital photography where pixels cost nothing (film did and took a lot out of the milk round pay!), making notes of where, what and train details for future reference, and being better able to compose pictures and see more in the frame than just the train (signal finials and station details for starters). Finally a realisation that it will all eventually change and disappear, and that if you don't make a record of it, it will go - forever! **BRM**

Preserved 5759 is seen at Shepherdswell on the East Kent Railway on May 24, 2009.

Inner end detail between the two cars showing the central buffer (fixed to DTS 77558), three-link coupling, brake hoses, roof access steps and high level control/electrical jumpers.

Choosing Addiscombe

With the new EMUs available from Bachmann and Hornby, **Gerrard Futtrell** looks at modelling a suitable third rail prototype.

Class 466 'Networker' EMU 466 011 waits to depart Addiscombe.

The majority of model railway layouts are based upon a freelance basic trackplan, with little or no attention given to its operation. But I have found from personal experience that using a known prototype and its operations as a basis, a convincing model railway layout can be based around it. Although in most cases it is not possible or even practical to create an accurate model of a specific prototype or station, with research and personal observation of the passenger and freight services a straight forward and sensible operating sequence can be devised without actually modelling the prototype station itself.

It has not been that often that I have come across an ideal prototype station, but on one such occasion, while travelling on a railtour, I was surprised to discover a station that I found more interesting than the locomotive that I was travelling behind! A station that would be a suitable prototype for a model railway layout on which to run my collection of proprietary models of old and new generation multiple units.

Addiscombe was a terminus station located in a residential area of Croydon, South London, being located at the end of a two mile branch line which left the Charing Cross-Hayes line at Elmers End. The station closed to traffic on May 31, 1997, after

being a part of the railway network for 133 years, a casualty of the Croydon Tramlink project.

The station was also a stabling point for the various types of EPB electric multiple units that could be found working the suburban services out of Charing Cross and Cannon Street. These were berthed in the station and carriage shed located opposite the station during the off-peak periods, and at weekends. The EPBs were withdrawn from service in the early to mid-1990s and replaced by Class 465 and 466 'Networker' units, although these were never berthed at this location.

A shuttle service operated every half an hour between Addiscombe and Elmers End. All through

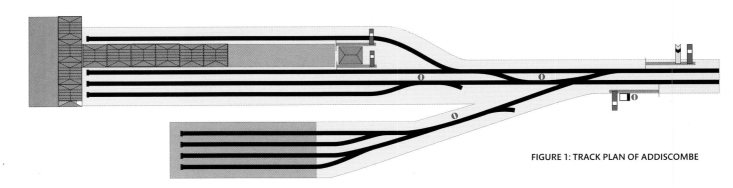

FIGURE 1: TRACK PLAN OF ADDISCOMBE

The view from the station looking towards Elmers End.

The SER signal box, later destroyed by fire in 1996.

services ceased in April 1976 with the station having closed to freight traffic from June 1968.

Addiscombe was also one of the last few remaining stations still to have semaphore signalling, although the rest of the branch line and local area was under the control of colour light signalling. The station still had a fine example of a South Eastern Railway wooden signal box until it was destroyed by fire in March 1996.

This has only been a brief outline and description of Addiscombe station. With the station track plan forming the basis of a model railway layout and an operating sequence devised around the regular shuttle service, a pleasing alternative modern layout could be realistically achieved. **BRM**

Addiscombe station looking towards the buffer stops.

Southern Substation

Graeme Elgar describes the role of this distinctive lineside feature and takes a look at the Bachmann Scenecraft model.

Barnham sub-station building. Note the replacement roller shutter door and modern signage (and more natural weathered concrete shade).

Barnham sub-station transformer enclosure. Note security chain link fencing with three strand barbed wire.

Halfway between the sub-stations there are Track Paralleling (TP) huts. Equipment within a TP hut is connected to the conductor rails and smooths out the current load between the adjacent sub-stations as the trains pass between them.

Hopefully this will give the reader a small insight as to how the former Southern Region of British Railways was electrically fed. All of the prototype photos accompanying this article were taken with permission and appropriate safety training.

The model

In 2011 Bachmann introduced a Lineside Transformer Site (44-043) to their Scalescene range to accompany their other Southern inspired buildings and EMUs. The model represents the design of sub-station built by the Southern Railway in the 1930s to serve their Portsmouth/Bognor Regis/Littlehampton/ Ore and Gillingham/ Maidstone schemes.

There are two parts to the model, these being the main building and the outside transformer, encased by chain link fencing with its high voltage cables, their concrete supports and associated insulators.

The building is a well-proportioned and detailed representation and comparing it to pictures of the installation at Barnham, there are a couple of detail differences, although other individual locations and their requirements along with alterations through time may well account for these, notably the large green wooden double doors, which have, at most locations now been replaced by roller shutters. The small glass tile windows are glazed and the decorative lines on the side have been captured well. The concrete colouring throughout both parts of the model

The Southern Railway third rail traction current of 750v DC is supplied to the conductor rail from lineside sub-stations. These receive current from a network of lineside cables which are fed from the National Grid at 33,000v AC *via* approximately 30 grid sub-stations.

Transformers in the lineside sub-stations step the high AC voltage down, which is rectified to 750v DC and fed through switchgear with circuit breakers to the conductor rails. These sub-stations are spaced at approximately three-mile intervals and are unmanned. They are, however, remotely supervised from the ten Electrical Control Rooms (ECR) strategically located around the region. The ECR operators can, if needed, remotely isolate power to sections of line for engineering work or in emergencies. Also if there are external supply problems to the system, power can be redistributed to the affected area *via* the lineside cables.

Side view of Bachmann's Lineside Transformer Site also known as a substation.

The transformer enclosure. Note slightly overscale chain link fencing!

...es appear a slightly 'suntanned' beige as ...posed to the more natural 'weathered ...ncrete' grey I found at Barnham, but this is a ...all criticism (and the colouring may well be ...ue to life at other locations).

The casting with the transformer, cables and ...ncrete supports is enclosed by chain link ...ncing topped with three strands of barbed ...re. The transformer is neatly modelled as are ...e insulators, high voltage cables and concrete ...pports. The chain link fencing is a perhaps a ...d overscale with 2mm squares (equal to 6"), ...d the 'barbed wire' more akin to heavy duty ...el cable. On my model one of the fence posts ...nt considerably off upright, but to be fair to ...chmann the above criticisms are only minor ...d not beyond the modeller to easily rectify.

Overall the model captures the 'Southern' feel ...the architecture and its purpose well, and I ...uld thoroughly recommend it to the growing ...mber of Southern electric modellers. *BRM*

The Bachmann casting in part of its packaging.

PRODUCT DETAILS
Bachmann SceneCraft: Lineside Transformer Site (44-043) priced £39.95

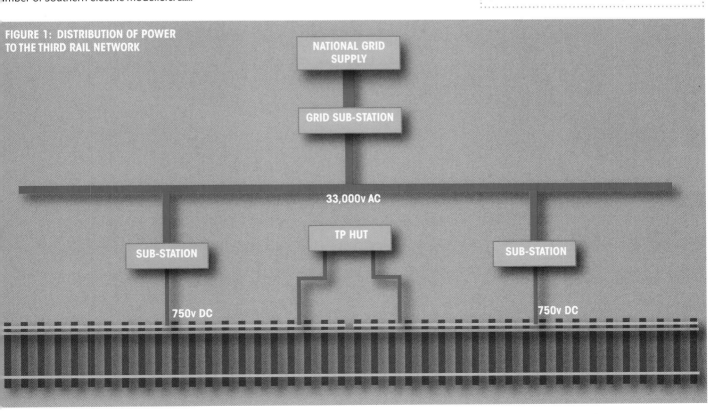

FIGURE 1: DISTRIBUTION OF POWER TO THE THIRD RAIL NETWORK

NATIONAL GRID SUPPLY

GRID SUB-STATION

33,000v AC

TP HUT

SUB-STATION

SUB-STATION

750v DC

750v DC

465 013 has just arrived at Hayes on a late morning working from Charing Cross on September 18, 2010. Note the station's neat well-kept appearance with recently installed seating and cycle racks.

Serving the suburbs

The neat, tidy south London suburban terminus of Hayes makes a suitable subject to model says **Martin Axford**. *Photography by the author.*

I had been a member of the Southern Railways Group for a number of years but never attended an AGM. However, in 2008 I decided to attend the meeting on impulse as it was at Hayes in South London. This meant a reasonably easy and quite interesting journey (part driving, part by train). I don't know what I was expecting but it's a good job I arrived early because Hayes station and its surroundings was a pleasant surprise. It had a clean canopied island platform and a neatly kept white painted station frontage which looked out onto a busy high street. This had a number of well cared-for mock Tudor shop fronts and a regular service of red-painted LT buses. I have prepared a number of articles

covering stations abroad but never thought I would feel inspired enough to cover a British subject!

A history of Hayes
The Elmers End to Hayes branch was originally built by the West Wickham & Hayes Railway. This company was absorbed by the South Eastern Railway when the line opened on May 29, 1882. At the time this part of North Kent was still rural in character, nevertheless the line was double-track from the start. Hayes station had a wide platform, a typical SER single storey wooden clapboard station building and a small goods yard. It even boasted a small turntable at the end of the main platform which must have

remained in use until electrification.

The SER and its arch rival in Kent, the London Chatham & Dover Railway, merged in 1898 to create the South Eastern & Chatham Railway. The creation of the SECR put a stop to wasteful competition and helped the new company to focus on important decisions like electrifying its suburban lines a few years later. Electrification took place after the Southern Railway had taken over in the 1920s using the LSWR inspired 660V dc third rail system. Meanwhile traffic had increased from that of a semi-rural line with a branch shuttle to that of an outer suburban line with through trains to Charing Cross.

A decade or so later in 1935 the station was totally rebuilt. The main platform was

On the same date, 465 152 arrives from Cannon Street.

lengthened considerably and became in effect an island platform. The track layout was simplified with the removal of the turntable, now not required with the use of double-ended electric multiple unit trains. The original building was swept away and replaced by the current functional though attractive structure incorporating a mini-concourse and passageway flanked by shops and offices.

During the war the building was badly damaged by a bomb but was eventually rebuilt in 1956 after the Southern had become part of the nationalised British Railways. The goods yard closed in 1965 but goods traffic was never very important on this line with household coal being the most important commodity. Most of the goods yard has been turned into the inevitable car park and lines not required for the intensive suburban service have been removed, leaving Hayes as just an island platform flanked by a line either side and a crossover clear of the platform end.

Despite this the station retains its distinctive 1930s character and seems to be kept in a very

376 022 at Hayes on September 12, 2008.

neat and tidy condition. In 1975 Hayes signal box was closed with the area coming under the control of London Bridge panel and with sectorisation in the '80s the Hayes branch became part of the Network South East empire.

In recent years the complex railway privatisation of the mid-1990s produced a situation in which split responsibility became the rule. This meant that the track and signals were owned first by Railtrack plc and now by Network Rail. The trains themselves were operated by a DoT appointed franchise, firstly Connex South Eastern and then by South Eastern. In 2004 the Strategic Rail Authority proposed to withdraw through trains to Charing Cross but were forced to back down when local councillors and the Hayes Village Association mounted a vigorous campaign. That brings us to the present situation with Hayes hopefully set to enjoy a frequent service to and from Central London for the foreseeable future.

Services and trains

Hayes probably enjoys a better service now than at any time in the past on weekdays and Saturdays. There are two departures at 12 and 42 minutes past each hour for Cannon Street, and at 27 and 57 minutes past each hour for Charing Cross with corresponding departures from both London stations. At peak times although there are more trains, they run to an irregular pattern with most services running to and from Charing Cross. On Sundays there are

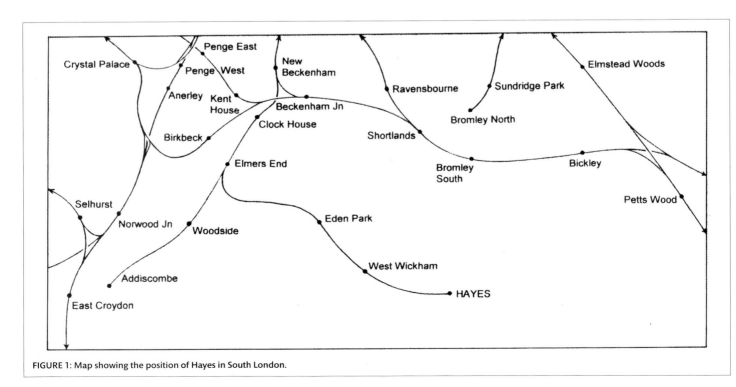

FIGURE 1: Map showing the position of Hayes in South London.

trains every 30 minutes to and from Charing Cross only.

Two types of EMU have been used. When I visited in September 2008 the 1990s-built Class 465s were in use on Cannon Street services with the 2004-built Class 376s being used on Charing Cross workings. So far 36 Class 376s have been built by Bombardier at Derby and are part of that company's 'Electrostar' production run, using the same bodyshell as the longer distance Class 375/377 units but without the corridor connection.

I found the situation had changed in September 2010, the Class 376s had been moved elsewhere and all services are now worked by 465 'Networkers'. 147 of these four-car units were built by BREL, ABB and Metro-Cammell from 1991 onwards. They are now reasonably reliable but when first introduced were plagued with teething troubles leading to a stay of execution for the reliable but very dated slam-door EPB units.

Until the introduction of newer types the Hayes branch was the exclusive domain of the ubiquitous EPB, large numbers of these tough reliable EMUs were built from 1951 onwards as both four and two-car sets. Earlier units had the curved SR Bulleid bodyside profile with the characteristic mini toplight above each door. Later units had the standard BR profile but were all built at BR's Eastleigh works with the same virtually flat unadorned cab ends giving them a very stark utilitarian appearance in contrast to their predecessors.

When the line was first electrified in the 1920s the Southern Railway ordered 55 new EMUs from Metropolitan-Cammell. Classified as 3-SUB by the Southern, 26 of these were for newly electrified Western section lines and had torpedo-ended cabs like previous LSWR units. Fortunately one vehicle from unit 1293 has been preserved at the National Railway

Above and left: The concourse area is a bit like an army barracks, but with the help of the clean skylight admitting the bright September sunshine and clear information displays it still looks reasonable.

unning for the train on September 18, 2010, at Hayes! Note the wall phone and ticket window in the dark dingy rridor linking the concourse with the station entrance. This corridor is the least attractive part of the station

Museum at York, beautifully finished in original lined SR green. The units intended for the Eastern section including the Hayes branch were very similar but had slightly flatter cabs. Before electrification and going back in time to SECR days, a Kitson-built steam railcar was tried on the Hayes-Elmers End shuttle for a few months in 1906, curiously predating the introduction of double-ended electric trains 20 years later. Other than this experiment services would have been worked by 'R', 'Q' and 'H' class 0-4-4T steam locomotives, coupled to sets of four or six-wheeled stock; bogie coaches were probably quite rare until electrification.

Ironically the Southern later built electric trains by using the bodies of such vehicles on new steel underframes and later, when EMUs became 'common user', would have been seen at Hayes.

Modelling possibilities

Unless you are genuinely interested in automatically controlled diorama type projects, I would suggest that the current track plan is too boring to make an interesting model. The accompanying 1942 plan could be used as a basis whatever period is being modelled. There are at least three possible scenarios in 4mm RTR: The current period could use the Hornby South Eastern livery Class 465 'Networker' unit for the frequent passenger services. The goods

The former goods yard has been turned into a very neat looking station car park - though it would be nicer to see freight trains rather than cars!

A passage provides direct access from the concourse to the car park and a ramp is thoughtfully provided for disabled passengers. Even the ubiquitous palisade fencing manages to look neat and tidy keeping the usual lines of 'wheelie-bins' in check

yard could be retained as a Permanent Way depot. Plenty of interesting items are available - the Hornby 'Seacow', 'Shark' and Heljan 'Mermaid' wagons come to mind. There are plenty of suitable locomotives - Bachmann's Class 66 is the obvious choice but a Bachmann or Vi-Trains Class 37 would also be suitable.

Going back to the '70s/'80s blue period would also be possible as DC Kits and Replica Railways produce excellent easily-assembled kits of the 4-EPBs. Again the goods yard could become a PW yard using the same vehicles already mentioned in earlier liveries but using Heljan Class 33s and Hornby/Lima Class 73s to pull them. Going back further still to the 1950s or '60s would still mean the use of the DC Kits/ Replica EPBs, this time painted green for the passenger service.

The goods yard could actually be modelled as such because it didn't close until 1965 and would mean modelling loose-coupled freight trains complete with a brake van pulled by the Class 33 or 73 in green, or maybe steam in BR black? Bachmann produce a very nice model of

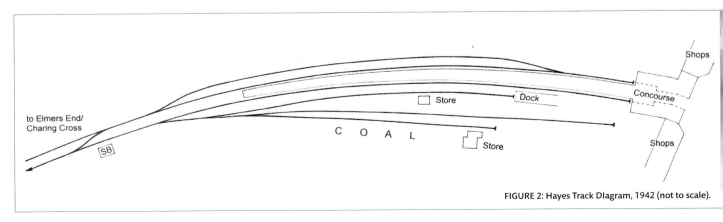

FIGURE 2: Hayes Track Diagram, 1942 (not to scale).

to Elmers End/ Charing Cross

SB

C O A L

Store

Dock

Store

Concourse

Shops

Shops

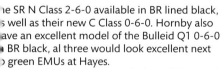

This view illustrates just how much has changed on many British stations - clean platform and canopy, decent modern seating, information and help points, and modern frequent trains.

Roadside view of Hayes station entrance on September 18, 2010, showing the excellent bus connections, good drop-off and pick-up facilities and the general ambience of the area.

he SR N Class 2-6-0 available in BR lined black, s well as their new C Class 0-6-0. Hornby also ave an excellent model of the Bulleid Q1 0-6-0 a BR black, al three would look excellent next o green EMUs at Hayes.

Peco make components which could be used o model the third rail system and the current 930s art-deco style station buildings are now vailable in the Bachmann Scenecraft range. he canopy may be a little more difficult but here are commercially available alternatives om Hornby and Airfix/Dapol if one wasn't too ussy. The main buildings don't have any omplicated roof shapes, in fact Hayes, Kent, is

one of the most attractive flat-roofed stations I have seen and deserves to be modelled.

Building a model of Hayes incorporating a goods yard of some sort would produce a very attractive and interesting layout which could be suitable for both home and exhibition use. Most of the rolling stock mentioned is either proprietary or easily assembled kit-built. Building a model of Hayes in the 1930s would need a lot more kit-building though it would still be possible.

It is intriguing to think that Hayes is now on its third generation of EMUs, one wonders what

the future holds for the line as trains already connect directly with the Croydon Tramlink at Elmers End. **BRM**

Further reading
- *An Historical Survey of Selected Southern Stations*
  G A Pryer & G J Bowring (OPC)

- *Southern Electric Album*
  Alan Williams (Ian Allan)

BR 4-SUB No.5146 arrives at Beckenham Junction on September 26, 1982.

ILLUMINATING
an Art Deco Signal Box

Graeme Elgar adds a detailed interior and lighting to the 4mm scale Bachmann Scenecraft model.

O ne of Bachmanns Southern inspired railway buildings in their Scenecraft range is an 'Art Deco' signal box. It follows the style of architecture favoured during the 1930s, not just by the Southern Railway, but also London Transport, shops and cinemas too. It was a bold departure from previous design styles with its use of concrete and large areas of glass to give a light and airy 'modern' feel. During the 1930s the Southern expanded its third rail electrification to reach Portsmouth, Maidstone and Gillingham and took the opportunity to carry out major infrastructure works such as rebuilding stations and renewing signalling and Permanent Way. Art Deco style signal boxes were built at several locations including Woking, Horsham, Portsmouth Harbour, Arundel, Bognor Regis, Swanley and Strood.

The Bachmann model is an excellent representation, capturing the detail well. Everything about it says 'Southern' and comparing it with pictures of Bognor and Horsham 'boxes, Bachmann have done very well! It does, however, lack one important element of detail – an interior and with all those windows it needs something! I not only gave the 'box an interior, but I gave it illumination too!

Bognor Regis signal box.

The Bachmann version, just out of the box!

The cold white interior suitably marked to show the extremes of the floor.

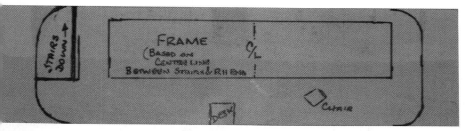

The 40thou styrene floor cut to 40 x 150mm showing the available floor space and where the frame and stairwell will go.

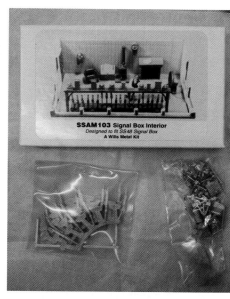

The Wills Signal box interior kit (SSAM103).

The casting is made of a white resin material, externally decorated, but internally plain white. To give the operating floor a 'railway feel' I painted the walls cream and the ceiling a coat of white. This also serves to lessen any light leakage and reduce the glare from the LEDs. The operating floor is 40mm (approx) x 25mm long. A piece of 40 thou styrene sheet was cut to 40mm x 150mm to allow for fixing and strength onto which I drew where I roughly wanted the interior equipment to go. Access to the operating floor is by a flight of stairs from ground level. With this in mind, the entry door to the signal box will be to the front and the stairs rise from ground level to a landing at the rear of the building, rising again up to the operating floor. Only the top half of the stairwell is modelled and I used half a staircase salvaged from an old Airfix/Dapol signal box kit backed with 10 thou styrene sheet. I marked out the stairwell and cut the floor to accommodate it later.

My signal box interior kit came from Wills which allows for a frame of 25 levers and includes various white metal castings for the signalman, block shelf, block instruments, a desk and an armchair. I bought two kits which allowed me to 'fill' the floor with a 40 lever frame. An aperture of 8mm x 120mm was cut from the floor (based on allowing 3mm for every lever for a 40 lever frame). The frame was installed, secured using Evo-Stick Impact adhesive and painted gloss black and the levers painted their various colours. Once the frame had dried, the floor was painted gloss 'lino' brown. Next the levers were installed in the frame, with most standing 'normal' (unpulled). I carried out a test fitting to make sure nothing was going to catch when being installed.

Next, measure the length of the frame and craft two block shelves together (the shelf in each kit is sufficient for a frame of 25 levers). When set, paint the shelf and supports (I used Pheonix Precision P129 BR Freight wagon bauxite). Also measure the distance between ceiling and operating floor, also the height of the levers. This is important as the legs of the block shelf need to be trimmed to just clear the

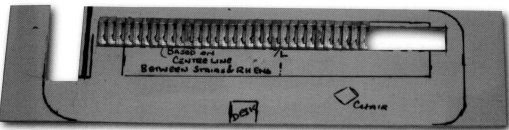

Building the frame in its 8mm x 120mm aperture with the stairwell cut out.

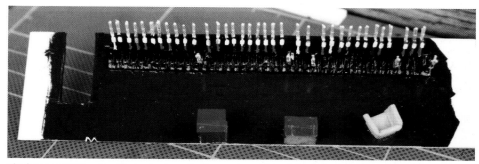

The frame complete with all levers in place - the lino has been laid and the desk and. most importantly. the armchair are in place.

top of the levers. A piece of styrene sheet needs to be cut to approximately 12mm x 30mm for the 'box diagram. Once glued to the block shelf, paint the back of the diagram brown and when dry carefully draw the track diagram on the front using a black permanent marker, adding signals where needed using a red marker (do it in that order as the ink takes a while to dry and is prone to smudging!). Paint and add the block instruments and block bells to the shelf. When it's all dry, install the block shelf.

Next paint the 10 thou styrene used for the staircase backing black and cut the staircase to fit (about five treads worth will suffice). Glue the styrene to the back of the stairs and trim to fit. Cut another piece of 10 thou styrene to the width of the stairs and allow approx 10mm - this will be the landing - and paint it black too. To support the floor I used three pieces of 80 thou styrene sheet cut to 40mm x 32mm and one of 32mm x 10mm. Paint two of the larger pieces cream on one side only. These will form

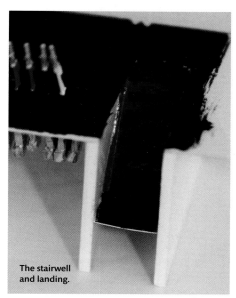

The stairwell and landing.

The interior of Bognor Regis signal box, showing the frame, blockshelf and diagram. The floor covering is grey here, this modern anti-slip covering replacing traditional brown polished linoleum earlier this century.

The blockshelf has been installed (still minus a block instrument though!) and our signalman is busy pulling a lever. There is an armchair, locker and desk and in between trains he's been busy with the polish on the lino!

: The LED strip has been fitted and the wires painted cream and made to run straight as if they were wiring conduits.

The resistors are soldered to a small piece of circuit board in series - apologies for the soldering – I know it'll never win awards!

the stairwell. The remaining large piece is placed at the other end of the frame and the smaller piece midway along the frame for intermediate support. Attach one piece of painted 40 x 32 sheet to the underside of the floor in line with the stairwell at the frame side. To this attach the stairs and landing, followed by the other side of the stairwell (when set, trim the landing to fit). Attach the small midway support halfway along the frame and the other piece of 32 x 40 at the other end of the frame.

One small detail added was the addition of the 'box cat seen sitting on the windowsill...

While all this is setting, it's time to turn to the illumination of the 'box. I chose self-adhesive strip LEDs. To disguise the wires, I used single strand bell wire, painted cream to pass as conduit piping. The LEDs were stuck to the ceiling towards the front of the 'box with the wires running down the inner wall between two windows. Cut two nicks out of the floor where the wires will pass through.

My 12 volt DC power source for the lighting is from the Tortoise point motor supply. During initial testing it became very apparent that some form of resistance would be needed as the 'box was lit up like a spaceship and there

was a large amount of light leakage through the structure itself. To overcome this I placed two 1K ½ Watt resistors (based on a 1 Amp supply) in series on the positive feed wire (soldered to a small piece of circuit board cut to fit the locking room interior). I tried resistors from Maplins, however, they were prone to overheating so I opted for much beefier ½ Watt specimens from Nairnshire Modelling Supplies which, after about six hours of continuous use, were still as cold as when I started! I also added Maplins Race Pack Leads (JG04E and JG05F - male and female connectors) to ease installation, and a simple on/off switch.

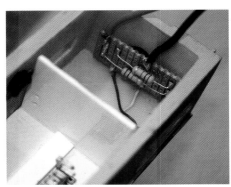

The circuit board has been neatly tucked out of the way, secured to the end wall of the locking room using bath seal adhesive.

The point rodding and signal wires exit slot at the base of Bognor Regis signal box, showing the concrete beam.

...e slot has been cut away and the raised brick detail
...moved from the four courses above for the concrete beam.

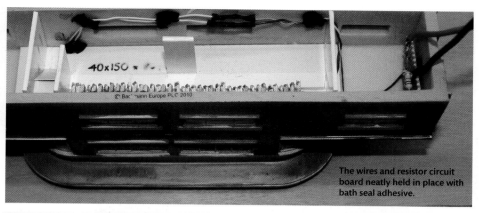

The wires and resistor circuit board neatly held in place with bath seal adhesive.

Looking at a photo of Bognor Regis 'box I
...alised I'd omitted an important part of the
...etail. A manual signal box must have an exit
...oint for the point rodding and signal wires. The
...achmann model does not have this on either
...de. At Bognor there is a long concrete beam
...hich rests upon two or three courses of
...rickwork, supporting the front wall of the 'box.
...n the model the walls are 5mm thick and the
...ick detail is raised. I decided to make the
...dding and wires slot 90mm long with the
...ntre line based on the frame, not the 'box, so
...does look slightly lopsided. I made a mark at
...ther end and gently scraped the brick detail
...om the two courses between those points to
...ow where the cut is to be made. Cut is
...rhaps a generous term for what happens next
...I had to gently scrape the material away until
...ad a uniform sized slot, which was finished
...th a light file. Care is needed during this stage
...d wear a protective mask to avoid inhaling
...y dust and hoover up the waste frequently.
...To represent the concrete beam I carefully
...easured 3mm each side of the slot and made
...ight score line over four courses of brickwork
...show the limits of the beam and the brick
...tail to be scraped away. I used an old craft
...ife blade to remove the raised brickwork and
...ve it a smooth finish with a rub over with a
...ass fibre pen, remembering to hoover away all
...e waste and give it all a rub down with a
...mp cloth. When happy with the end result, I

A daytime view of the lit interior with the 'box cat looking on!

painted the beam weathered concrete.
To prevent any light leakage from the newly
created slot I covered the rear of the aperture
with a piece of styrene sheet, ready for the
rodding detail to be added when the ballasting
has been completed.
With the interior ready, the floor/interior was
slid into position. The underfloor wiring was
then secured to the walls of the locking room
using bath seal adhesive (pic ADSB18)
A 16mm hole was drilled through the
baseboard for the wires and connector to pass
through and the 'box placed in position. **BRM**

Useful Contacts:
• **Bachmann Europe:**
www.bachmann.co.uk
• **Maplins:** www.maplins.co.uk
• **Nairnshire Modelling Supplies:**
PO Box 6078, Nairn IV12 5WU
www.nairnshire-modelling-supplies.co.uk
• **Langley Models:**
166, Three Bridges Road, Three Bridges,
Crawley, West Sussex RH10 1LE
www.langley-models.co.uk]

...he 'box lit up showing the lit
...nterior and the point rodding/
...ignal wires exit slot.

Oxminster High Level station.

OXMINSTER *REVISITED*

Following a visit by Tony Wright a couple of years ago, **Stephen Sindle** brings us up to date with progress on his layout. *Photos by the author.*

They always say that a model railway is never finished and Oxminster is no exception. I suppose after a certain period of operating I got itchy feet (or should that be fingers?), so the planning got under way and the end result was the remodelled Oxminster.

First of all there was the transformation from the Oxminster that first appeared in the July 2008 issue of *British Railway Modelling*. The first thing was the removal of the two main platforms and construction of the viaduct which effectively covered the entire area of the original Platforms 1 and 2, leaving Platform 3 as it was except for the relocation of the platform buildings from Platform 1 to Platform 3. Next an island platform was built on top of the viaduct which was designed as a Beeching era 'cut'; in other words the line terminated at the platform end but the track bed continues onwards under a bridge to the scenic backdrop, is overgrown and the original starting signal post, which is still *in situ*, is now rusting. At the other end of the station the line crosses the street near the original station building over a level crossing as a single line at this point, and therefore the station names were changed slightly to Oxminster High Level and Low Level to reflect this.

Oxminster High Level with a DMU awaiting departure time.

Oxminster Central in 1966 - local suburban services are still steam hauled but the third rail is down and ready.

yard/storage sidings has worked for me mainly because most of the stock is stored away and not left on the layout; exceptions being the CEPs and EPB due to the difficulty in uncoupling the units after every operating session.

With this revamp of the railway I relaid the conductor rail from scratch. This time the correct Peco rail and chairs/pots were used but there was still a problem as Lima and Hornby Class 73 locos fouled it! The only way I was able to operate them was by removing the sand pipes from the bogies and filing down some of the moulding round the fuel tanks and compressors. Prior to the relaying of the third rail I thought it was me, as I had used N gauge rail and not that which was recommended. But this made only a minor difference as previously it had only affected some steam locos with their brake gear rubbing on the top of the third rail. I would be interested to know if any one else has found this problem.

Location

The previous Oxminster was located towards the south west and had some vague connections with the S&D in some of its operations. But here, in the true spirit of model railways and artistic licence, we find ourselves further east and truly in third rail country.

What we have to visualise is that the railway

Next to be changed was the area of the storage sidings which were very much under-used, as most of the time I only ever had the items of rolling stock actually in use on the layout at any one time.

So the thought of another scenic area came to mind and the new station of Oxminster Central was conceived. This consists of a four platform station with a small diesel servicing shed beside it. The scenic break at one end is an overbridge carrying the main road with the carriage shed in low relief extending under and supposedly beyond the bridge. The station signal box is beside the shed and the over bridge. The station's two centre roads are the terminal platforms with the through lines passing either side of them.

The usual materials were used in the construction of the station, a Metcalfe kit for the buildings and platforms although in a bespoke way with the canopies all being Dapol kits. The carriage shed was constructed from a Superquick bus garage kit, altered to suit the requirements for the diesel stabling point. Signalling is by Ratio kits built to prototypical arrangements to suit their location.

I think really this was the main purpose behind the last part of the alterations - to be able to run the Bachmann 4-CEP and other units back and forth from the main station to the two roads under the viaduct where the old station platforms used to be, which in part had become storage sidings in their own right (as they are now all out of sight). This part could now be described as 'out and back' and of course the new high level part of the layout operates in the same way.

Well I think Oxminster has evolved as much as it can, next time there is only the option of a new layout and a new theme. I like this revised railway myself, although I appreciate that some of you may think it to be a little over the top or too crowded. The removal of the fiddle

The Oxminster Central Station pilot is still a steam loco in 1968.

A DMU departs from Oxminster High Level.

A general view of Oxminster Central including the depot.

OXMINSTER TRACK PLAN

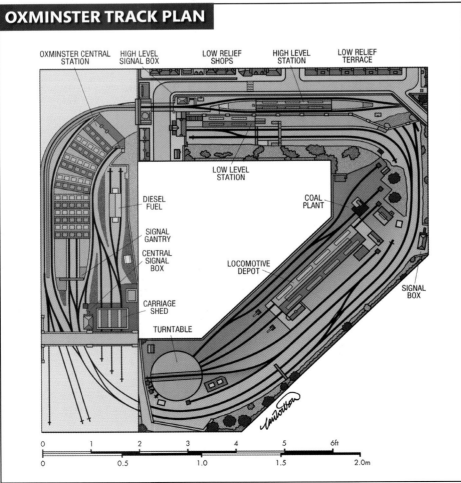

OXMINSTER CENTRAL STATION

HIGH LEVEL SIGNAL BOX

LOW RELIEF SHOPS

HIGH LEVEL STATION

LOW RELIEF TERRACE

LOW LEVEL STATION

DIESEL FUEL

SIGNAL GANTRY

CENTRAL SIGNAL BOX

CARRIAGE SHED

TURNTABLE

COAL PLANT

LOCOMOTIVE DEPOT

SIGNAL BOX

0   1   2   3   4   5   6ft

0   0.5   1.0   1.5   2.0m

by the loco depot is actually two parallel single lines which start at Oxminster Junction. The junction box controls the point at which three lines come together; the two single lines and the end/start of a double track main line. The two single lines go past the loco depot and under the bridge (at this point we lose about half a mile of line) for the other side of the bridge brings us to Oxminster Central Station. Here the two single lines can be crossed to access the terminal platforms. The two single lines then go their separate ways off to the rest of the railway! Returning to Oxminster Junction, the lines again divide; one of the routes forks left to Oxminster Low Level single line platform station with the small addition of a turn-about platform beside it to save terminating services on the single line and returning back from where they came. The two other lines (the Up and Down line) disappear through the tunnel and onwards. Another single line branches to the right through another tunnel portal and away to elsewhere (sorry if that's a bit vague, but use your imagination as I do!). In a nutshell there are three routes converging here to form single or reversible lines from Oxminster Junction to Central station. Most of the lines are electrified by the third rail although two lines are not - the branch through the single tunnel and the avoiding line at Central station.

The High Level platforms at Oxminster are effectively the truncated remains of another through line which now provide a commuter link from the island platform over the level crossing and cross country to a main line connection, this is also a non-electrified route.

In truth, such a location would never have existed (well not after nationalisation at least), such a network of routes in such a small location could only be the results of private railway companies competing in pre-grouping days which would be totally non-viable today, but it makes for interesting operations with a mix of traffic and different time eras as well.

Operation

This brings us to operation. This can be steam on loco-hauled services with some diesel hauled services and a DMU pottering back and forth on other services representing the end of steam era (1960-67); through to the latest era (late 1970s) with loco-hauled services in the minority and multiple units performing most services, be that EMU or DMU. As mentioned above the 4-CEPs and 2-EPBs form the shuttle from the terminal platforms at Central station and Class 108, 110, 101 and 117 units run all other services. The loco shed does see changes, but only in the motive power using it rather than any rebuilding of the site. BR has seen fit to let the infrastructure remain as it was at the end of steam, although no doubt plans for closure or rebuilding of the depot must be on the cards.

New order at Oxminster Central - the station is full of EMUs.

Signalling

At Oxminster Junction Box the two single lines and the double track main are all seen to be controlled by early examples of three aspect colour light signals which had replaced the original semaphores.

At Oxminster Central the signals are all semaphore and the starting signals on the station gantry make a pretty impressive sight, mainly because of the fact that the lines heading away from Oxminster Central are both parallel single lines, with the means of accessing either line from all platforms.

At Oxminster High Level the signalling is pretty basic as there is just a single line running in to two platforms both of which are signalled for return working.

Again I have to thank the family for putting up with my absence as I pursued the remodelling of the railway to the detriment of the garden at times as it dragged on into what should be a non-railway season! **BRM**

Oxminster, Main Street level crossing.

Oxminster, 1967 and the London service is still in the hands of steam!

2-HAL No.2633, built in 1939 for the Medway electrification scheme, is seen at Earlsfield on April 12, 1964. *J Phillips/Colour-Rail.com /210855 1939*

A fast finish

Andy Hopper builds a 4mm scale resin 2-HAL EMU from a Southern Region/Ajay Models kit. *Photography by the author.*

I've built electric multiple units for Canterbury MRS Chairman Dennis Prior's third rail layout Abbots Barton from brass, aluminium, plastic, and various combinations of them from several different manufacturers. It has to be said that the quality of some of the kits is better than others. I was

therefore very interested when he asked if I'd build a new resin 2-HAL kit from Southern Region Models/Ajay Models, a manufacturer that I had not come across before. They told me it would be quick and simple to build as each coach body was in one piece, with interior, underframe, and bogies also as one

piece mouldings.

I've only built half a dozen loco kits from resin, but this experience suggested that the castings sometimes warp when they come out of the moulds, so I looked quite carefully at the coach mouldings before the kit was bought – if they were banana shaped then it would have been very difficult to make anything of the kit. They all looked pretty straight, so money changed hands, and I was committed.

Building started with cleaning off the flash. There was actually not very much. Most of the window openings had a thin film of resin across them, this was removed by running a sharp scalpel blade lightly around the openings and then gently scraping the blade around the inside, and finishing with fine wet and dry paper. The lower edge of the body was lightly filed, and that was the preparation of the body done. Here, however, a word of warning – the fine dust from the filing made my hands itch, so from then on I wore latex gloves when handling the resin. I always wear these gloves when paint spraying so that I can hold things in one hand and spray with the other and keep my hands clean. I get the gloves from my friendly local vet, a box of 100 only costs about £7.50.

The interior moulding was not quite so good. After the corridor windows were cleaned out, a little filing was needed to straighten and square up the openings, and the corridor partition was quite rough in places. Some of

The completed unit seen from the front.

Have your say! Visit our new Forum at: **www.RMweb.co.uk**

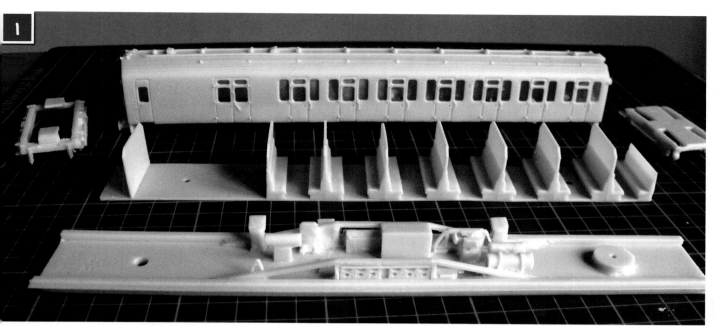

All of the parts of one coach – there really are very few.

he seats had dimples in, but I didn't do anything about this as they would be invisible once they were inside the coach and only seen through the small Bulleid windows. The underframe had little flash, but the horizontal parts of the trusses were rather warped. I tried bending them straight with my fingers without success, then heated them with a hair dryer before straightening them, but again they just went back to their original shape, so I cut out the bent parts and replaced them with Evergreen strip fixed in with superglue. The holes for the bolts to hold on the bogies were opened up so that the top of the bolt did not protrude above the floor.

The bogies also needed a little cleaning up. This was quite fiddly as some of the gaps here were rather small. I used a fine (about 0.6mm or so) drill bit in a pin chick as a scraper, and that worked well. Overall this cleaning up process took only about an hour per coach. The next stage was a good scrub with a toothbrush and Cif' cleaner, and a thorough rinse to get rid of all the grease and swarf. The photos show the before and after condition of the various bits.

Adding the detail
What little detailing that's needed came next. Door handles and handrails are not provided, but there are holes for them (with all the detail on the body I wonder why the door handles are not moulded in too?). For door handles I usually use brass pins with the heads ground flat using a mini drill and grinding wheel, this gives a sturdier result than etched ones, and something that's large enough to see and handle with ease. These are superglued into the holes, and then cut off flush on the inside. If you prefer etched door handles then they are available from firms such as Roxey Mouldings. The cut off parts of the pins were used to make the handrails (waste not, want not!) – they are a little thicker than I would normally use, but seemed to fit in well with the moulded-on detail here. To get the size right I bent one end at right angles, put that in one of the fixing holes, then gripped the pin with pliers just

A thin film of resin needs to be removed from the window openings.

The front end showing all of the detail moulded in – a great time saver.

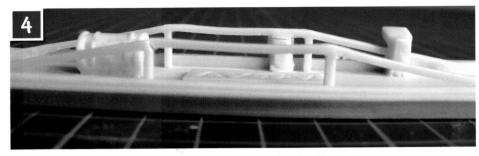

The warped underframe trusses which had to be cut out and replaced in plastic.

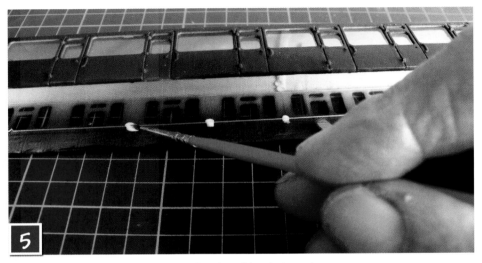

Applying drops of 'Micro Krystal Klear' to the edge of the glazing strip.

until later than the period of the layout.
Painting and glazing
In the paint shop

Next came another wash, and after drying thoroughly, a visit to the paint shop where all the parts were sprayed with Halfords grey primer. After checking for faults the bogies and underframes were sprayed with Halfords matt black, and the interior mouldings brush painted with Humbrol acrylics as recommended in the instructions. The footboards were painted dark brown to represent wood. The body sides were then airbrushed with Railmatch Southern EMU green acrylic paint, and the ends brush painted with Tamiya 'Nato Black' acrylic. I'm quite sure there is a car paint spray which matches SR green and make painting much easier, but as I'm partially colour blind I can't pick it out! If anyone out there can identify matching colours, write to the Editor who I'm sure would publish them. Modern day car sprays are fuss free and give a very good quality finish.

Transfers were applied next. I have a good stock of Modelmasters, but there are a number of other good makes too. Then all was finished off with Games Workshop 'Purity Seal' satin varnish. This gives a very good finish, but be warned that it should only be applied over acrylic paint as it makes a splendid job of stripping enamel - I was pretty upset when I found this out the hard way on another project! The last paint job was the roof, in a matt dark grey, I didn't want this varnished as it

where the bend has to come, carefully pull the pin out of the body without altering the grip of the pliers, and bend the pin again, making sure that both the bent down ends are parallel and at right angles to the main section of the handrail. If it comes out wrong, don't bother to try to correct it, or force it into the holes, it's much quicker in the long run (as I know from bitter experience) just to throw it away and start again. The pictures show this process on a plain piece of plastic as it was easier to photograph it this way. When gluing to the body, space the handrail away from the body side with a thin piece of card to make sure they are all consistent. Finally the roof mounted air horns were removed by snipping with side cutters, then filing flat as these were not fitted

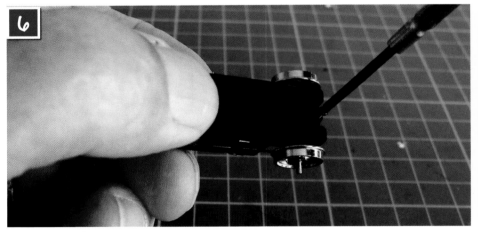

Unscrewing the keeper on the 'Spud' motor bogie to change the wheels.

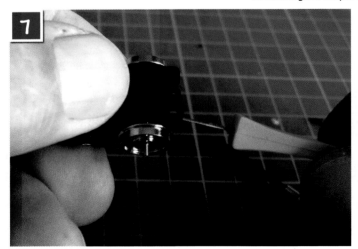

Carefully levering it off with a scalpel blade – mind your fingers!

Setting the back-to-back gauge on the new wheelset. The gear has already been put on the axle.

should look just a little grubby.

When the paint was dry the glazing was fitted. I felt the strip provided in the kit was a bit on the flimsy side, so I used strips of slightly thicker acrylic sheet which I keep for this sort of thing. I find acrylic better than clear polystyrene as it is less prone to scratching, you should be able to find it at a good exhibition. I like to use a product called 'Micro Kristal Klear' for sticking in the glazing. It is a PVA glue which dries absolutely clear. I find the best way is to put the glazing in place, and put spots of glue along the edge in line with the gaps between the windows to keep it as far away from the visible areas as possible. A small weight will keep everything tight while it all sets.

Motor and trailing bogies

With all of this done it was time to fit the bogies. Hornby coach wheels were sprung into place (check the back-to-back measurement if you use fine scale track as they tend to be a bit tight for that), and short lengths of 0.7mm brass wire were glued to the top of the stretcher, running side to side on one bogie and front to back on the other (see photo 11). This allows a slight rock to accommodate irregularities in the track.

The motor bogie was next. I was given a Tenshodo 'Spud' from Branchlines. The wheels were very small, so larger wheels were also provided, and had to be fitted, easily done in accordance with the Tenshodo instructions. After this had been completed the pinpoints on the ends of the axles had to be cut off – I used a strong pair of side cutters followed by a file to smooth off the rough bits. I've always hesitated to use a cutting disc in a mini drill in case the heat generated melts the plastic insulation causing the wheel to go out of round.

The resin coach floor is too thick for the Tenshodo mounting screw to be used, so I used a bolt instead. As this didn't have such a large head I stuck one of the spacers supplied with the bogie centrally over the hole. Take care when doing this as if the bolt is too long and is screwed too far into the bogie it jams the motor (I found out the hard way and had to find a shorter one).

And finally...

Finally the coaches were coupled with a hook and bar made from brass wire, and there you have it. A very acceptable two-car unit in a

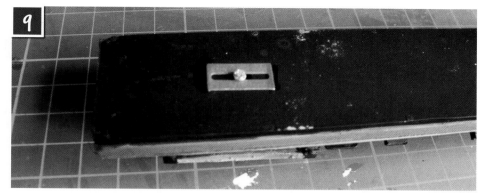

The spacer glued over the fixing hole so that an ordinary bolt can be used to attach the 'Spud'.

The 'Spud' reassembled with the new, bigger wheels.

Wires were glued to the bogie tops to give a little flexibility to the riding of the coaches.

very short time (for kit building). I'm afraid that I rather lost track of just how long it took, as I was involved in other projects too, but I would think no more than six hours should have covered it. These kits won't give you a hi-fi rendition of your favourite unit to go in a glass case, but give a most acceptable 'layout unit' as defined by Tony Wright. **BRM**

> **FURTHER READING**
> • *An Historical Survey of Selected Southern Stations* by G A Pryer & G J Bowring (OPC)
>
> • *Southern Electric Album* by Alan Williams (Ian Allan)

The finished unit from the side.

A better club newsletter

For over eight years **David Coasby** was editor of the MRC's *Bulletin*. Here he reveals the secrets of what makes a good club newsletter.

Photography by the author.

I suspect a large majority of readers are members of a model railway club or society, and these can vary from just a dozen or so members up to several hundred.

One of the problems such organisations have is keeping members informed, as in many cases they can live long distances from where the club or society is based and can't always attend on a regular basis. But it's important to keep their interest alive and their membership active as without this they are likely to leave and in most cases their annual subscription lost.

Newsletters are nothing new. I've seen some great ones, and I have to say, some terrible ones. Most inform, but some look so boring and are printed so badly they give a bad impression of that organisation. And it's not just a question of cost. It doesn't actually cost any less to print a bad newsletter than it does to print a good one! Although I've spent most of my working life as a graphic designer you don't need all the 'bells and whistles' I use professionally to produce a good looking newsletter for your club, particularly as most of us now have access to a computer and there are lots of different software that anyone can use – some of which is free.

I'm not about to give you an ABC on how to make your newsletter the best thing since sliced bread, but hopefully guide you through a few things worth considering, and just as important, a few things not worth thinking about.

Page size

Lets start with size. The actual content (the text and photographs you want to publicise) will dictate the number of pages. Remember here that unless it's a very simple two-sided sheet, then the number of pages must be in combinations of four (four, eight, twelve and so on) as this is how a printer will produce the document.

The actual page size is the next consideration. A4 (297mm x 210mm) and A5 (210mm x 148mm) are the two most popular and common sizes, easily handled by any printer. Both have their advantages and both have their disadvantages. A4, being the larger (it's the same size as most letters you receive) allows more space per page to lay out your text and photographs, but can cost more to post. An A5 document will fit a smaller envelope and therefore cost less to post (weight permitting).

However, when I produced the *Bulletin* for The Model Railway Club in London we compromised. I just love the versatility that an A4 format gives, but the Club's Committee don't like the cost of the postage. Simple solution: we folded the *Bulletin* in half so that it fits the smaller envelope. A bit of a nuisance, but it has established a truce between myself and the Committee!

Font (typeface) style

The next consideration is the font and sizes used. Just because you've discovered your computer has hundreds of them please don't be tempted to use them all - it will look like a dog's dinner! I like to keep to a plain sans font for headings and usually have them all the same size – 24 point. Sub headings are again in the same font, but obviously smaller - I use 14 point.

The font chosen for the main text is very subjective. Simply choose one you like but one that is clean and legible. Don't go for one of the whacky ones - it doesn't work! All my main text is the same font and size of 10 point with any emphasis being made in italic or the bold version of the same font. 'Times' or 'Arial' are both good fonts, versatile and widely available both on PC or Mac, though I use 'Myriad' because this is the chosen corporate font we use at the MRC. Ten point text is a readable size for most folk and one must consider that a large part of most club's membership are possibly elderly, so they may have impaired eyesight. Out of interest I produce design work for my local council and their minimum text size is 12 point, as recommended by the RNIB. But magazines such as *BRM* and others use smaller sizes, so it's something you need to consider.

The other main styling requirement for text is whether the text is 'ranged left' as used in the *Bulletin* (and on this page) or 'justified'. Personally I find 'ranged left' style easier to read and it avoids the large spaces you sometimes get between words when text is 'justified'. But it's a subjective issue, so maybe try out a few different styles and sizes and see what friends have to say.

The newsletter banner should be distinctive. Our's includes the name, the Club's logo and below, edition number and other details.

The use of a larger bolder intro paragraph helps draw the reader into the rest of the article.

The saying goes that a picture speaks a thousand words. Always try to have an interesting image on the outer cover. There's nothing more visually boring than a page of plain text - and remember to credit the photographer (even if it's yourself)!

The BULLETIN

The bi-monthly newsletter of The Model Railway Club (www.themodelrailwayclub.org)   Number 464 © January / February 2012

PLATFORM

We had a useful informal discussion after the business part of the AGM, and amongst the topics was 'subscriptions' and 'membership'. I had remarked that the Committee had made a decision to avoid a subscription increase, but to take a positive step to increase membership numbers. Increasing numbers means exposing the Club more in the hobby: (i) by attending more exhibitions, both with layouts (MRC's own and member's layouts under the MRC 'flag') and our own 'roadshows'; (ii) by getting more articles into the hobby press; (iii) by continuing with our tradition of producing a great Annual Exhibition and 'Open Day'; (iv) by making sure our Lectures and other events are fully publicised through both the hobby press and our website.

Having made people aware that we exist and are very much alive, potential members will come to Keen House, and there was a lot of discussion about how folk are introduced to the Club, and several positive ideas are being acted upon already.

But increasing membership is one thing, then there is the challenge to retain those new members! That often means providing some focus on projects, and I would say that the OO layout will become very much more accessible once the essential re-wiring is completed by Bob, Manus & Sam, and much more needs to be done to get the layout ready for our March show. It is great that other people are getting involved now. The HO layout with regular operating sessions is moving firmly ahead as it goes 'round the bend' of the

projected oval. We are also hoping to have a new Gauge O demonstration layout on the Club stand at 'Ally Pally'. Equally importantly I was very excited at the strong response to creating an EM gauge layout at Keen House following Duncan Redford's proposal at the AGM (for details contact Duncan directly – duncan.redford@nmrn.org.uk – or myself). We will be building on our experiences of the 'Modelling In Focus' (MiF) groups started in the Spring once we are properly into the New Year which gives us the informal but focussed modelling sessions/ demonstrations on Thursdays, and with more equipment in the workshop downstairs – including the now refurbished Collet Lathe and the new Resistance Soldering Unit (RSU) there are greater opportunities there.

I do thank my friends and colleagues in the Club for your support during my first year in the 'hot seat' at the MRC. To the retiring members of the Committee I again say Thank You, and to the new Committee – Yes we have challenges but we will continue to develop and build on what has been laid down before, but not to be frightened of new ideas. Whilst for some reason we did not manage to have elections at the recent AGM, let me say that we are always open for new ideas at any level in the MRC. 'Ordinary' members often have many skills and specialist areas of interests, and we are always glad of input, and can co-opt folk on to the Committee when needed...

In conclusion to this the 100th Year of The Model Railway Club, it only remains for me to wish all of our members, friends and associates in the hobby, the very best for 2012.

Leslie Bevis-Smith *Chairman*

Brrrrrrr! What a fantastic winter-time shot taken during World War II of one of the Classification Yards of the Chicago and North Western Railroad, Chicago, December 1942. Photo: Jack Delano

MRC Bulletin No. 464   January/February 2012   **1**

Here we see two columns. Most of the pages in the *Bulletin* usually comprise the more versatile three-column format, but on every edition on the second page we list the Club's contact details and the editorial, where two columns are more suited.

Note the use of a light coloured panel as an aid to keeping the two articles separate and adding visual interest to a page which only contains text.

Don't forget to inform your readers when your next copy date is due and remind them how to contact you, email, address etc.

It's a nice touch to include the printers name and phone number. They will appreciate the publicity and are more likely to do a good job if they know their name is on it!

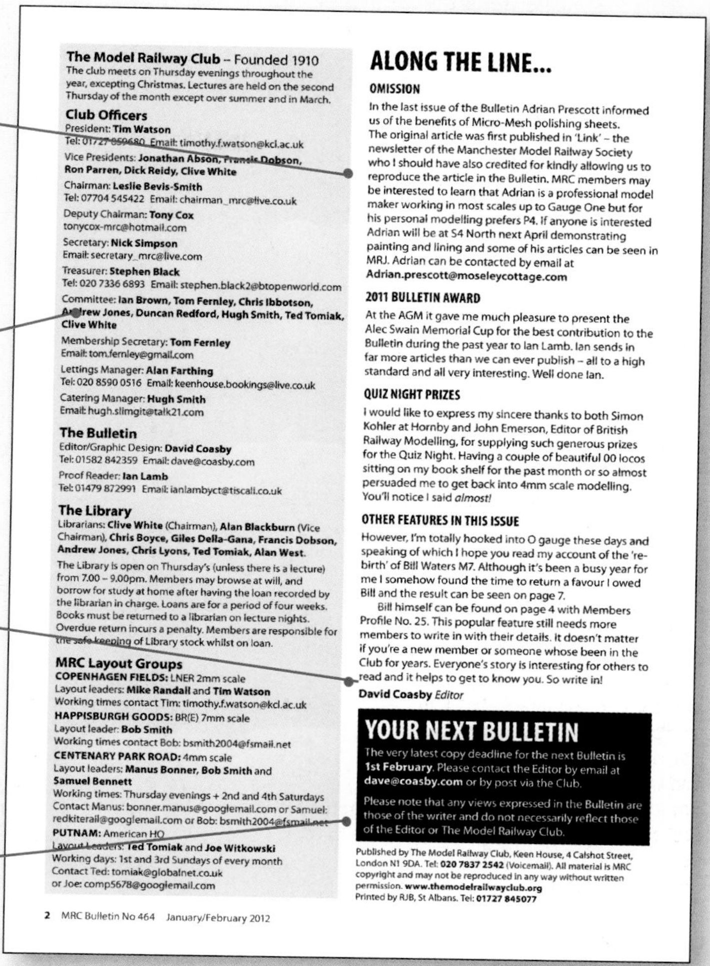

The Model Railway Club – Founded 1910
The club meets on Thursday evenings throughout the year, excepting Christmas. Lectures are held on the second Thursday of the month except over summer and in March.

Club Officers
President: **Tim Watson**
Tel: 01727 859680 Email: timothy.f.watson@kcl.ac.uk
Vice Presidents: **Jonathan Abson, Francis Dobson, Ron Parren, Dick Reidy, Clive White**
Chairman: **Leslie Bevis-Smith**
Tel: 07704 545422 Email: chairman_mrc@live.co.uk
Deputy Chairman: **Tony Cox**
tonycox-mrc@hotmail.com
Secretary: **Nick Simpson**
Email: secretary_mrc@live.com
Treasurer: **Stephen Black**
Tel: 020 7336 6893 Email: stephen.black2@btopenworld.com
Committee: **Ian Brown, Tom Fernley, Chris Ibbotson, Andrew Jones, Duncan Redford, Hugh Smith, Ted Tomiak, Clive White**
Membership Secretary: **Tom Fernley**
Email: tom.fernley@gmail.com
Lettings Manager: **Alan Farthing**
Tel: 020 8590 0516 Email: keenhouse.bookings@live.co.uk
Catering Manager: **Hugh Smith**
Email: hugh.slimgit@talk21.com

The Bulletin
Editor/Graphic Design: **David Coasby**
Tel: 01582 842359 Email: dave@coasby.com
Proof Reader: **Ian Lamb**
Tel: 01479 872991 Email: ianlambyct@tiscali.co.uk

The Library
Librarians: **Clive White** (Chairman), **Alan Blackburn** (Vice Chairman), **Chris Boyce, Giles Della-Gana, Francis Dobson, Andrew Jones, Chris Lyons, Ted Tomiak, Alan West.**
The Library is open on Thursday's (unless there is a lecture) from 7.00 – 9.00pm. Members may browse at will, and borrow for study at home after having the loan recorded by the librarian in charge. Loans are for a period of four weeks. Books must be returned to a librarian on lecture nights. Overdue return incurs a penalty. Members are responsible for the safe keeping of Library stock whilst on loan.

MRC Layout Groups
COPENHAGEN FIELDS: LNER 2mm scale
Layout leaders: **Mike Randall** and **Tim Watson**
Working times contact Tim: timothy.f.watson@kcl.ac.uk
HAPPISBURGH GOODS: BR(E) 7mm scale
Layout leader: **Bob Smith**
Working times contact Bob: bsmith2004@fsmail.net
CENTENARY PARK ROAD: 4mm scale
Layout leaders: **Manus Bonner, Bob Smith** and **Samuel Bennett**
Working times: Thursday evenings + 2nd and 4th Saturdays
Contact Manus: bonner.manus@googlemail.com or Samuel: redkiterail@googlemail.com or Bob: bsmith2004@fsmail.net
PUTNAM: American HO
Layout Leaders: **Ted Tomiak** and **Joe Witkowski**
Working days: 1st and 3rd Sundays of every month
Contact Ted: tomiak@globalnet.co.uk
or Joe: comp5678@googlemail.com

ALONG THE LINE...

OMISSION
In the last issue of the Bulletin Adrian Prescott informed us of the benefits of Micro-Mesh polishing sheets. The original article was first published in 'Link' – the newsletter of the Manchester Model Railway Society who I should have also credited for kindly allowing us to reproduce the article in the Bulletin. MRC members may be interested to learn that Adrian is a professional model maker working in most scales up to Gauge One but for his personal modelling prefers P4. If anyone is interested Adrian will be at S4 North next April demonstrating painting and lining and some of his articles can be seen in MRJ. Adrian can be contacted by email at **Adrian.prescott@moseleycottage.com**

2011 BULLETIN AWARD
At the AGM it gave me much pleasure to present the Alec Swain Memorial Cup for the best contribution to the Bulletin during the past year to Ian Lamb. Ian sends in far more articles than we can ever publish – all to a high standard and all very interesting. Well done Ian.

QUIZ NIGHT PRIZES
I would like to express my sincere thanks to both Simon Kohler at Hornby and John Emerson, Editor of British Railway Modelling, for supplying such generous prizes for the Quiz Night. Having a couple of beautiful 00 locos sitting on my book shelf for the past month or so almost persuaded me to get back into 4mm scale modelling. You'll notice I said *almost!*

OTHER FEATURES IN THIS ISSUE
However, I'm totally hooked into O gauge these days and speaking of which I hope you read my account of the 're-birth' of Bill Waters M7. Although it's been a busy year for me I somehow found the time to return a favour I owed Bill and the result can be seen on page 7.
Bill himself can be found on page 4 with Members Profile No. 25. This popular feature still needs more members to write in with their details. It doesn't matter if you're a new member or someone whose been in the Club for years. Everyone's story is interesting for others to read and it helps to get to know you. So write in!
David Coasby *Editor*

YOUR NEXT BULLETIN
The very latest copy deadline for the next Bulletin is **1st February**. Please contact the Editor by email at **dave@coasby.com** or by post via the Club.
Please note that any views expressed in the Bulletin are those of the writer and do not necessarily reflect those of the Editor or The Model Railway Club.

Published by The Model Railway Club, Keen House, 4 Calshot Street, London N1 9DA. Tel: **020 7837 2542** (Voicemail). All material is MRC copyright and may not be reproduced in any way without written permission. **www.themodelrailwayclub.org**
Printed by RJB, St Albans. Tel: **01727 845077**

2 MRC Bulletin No 464 January/February 2012

he banner heading
ere is one exception where you can ometimes use one of those 'odd-ball' fonts to ood effect if you so wish. You need to create n individual look to your newsletter and the anner at the top of the front page needs to eflect this, though I'd avoid making it too fussy. ake a look in your local newsagent and judge hich ones work best, but remember you're ot trying to compete with a national magazine at is marketed with a huge budget.

he cost of producing the document
his brings me onto that important subject of roduction costs. Chances are that your club or ociety want you to produce the best possible esult for the least amount of money (I don't now of any who don't). Hopefully you already wn a computer and some sort of software that suitable. The time you spend producing the ocument is no doubt being given free – so no osts so far!

Sometimes you will see a picture you want to se from a photographic website or on Google, tc. Many are copyright restricted so don't try o copy them or you could end up in trouble. lost of the photographic website images re available for sale at very varying fees. ut if, like me, you work with a zero budget or such items then that may appear to be a o-no. However, I have found that if there is a articular image you really must have, an email o the photographer can help. Explaining who ou are, what you are producing and the fact at it is just for your Club's membership, with o commercial sale, will sometimes result in the hotographer granting you a one-off free use f their image, providing you add a credit in the icture caption – something along the lines of 'hotograph kindly provided by A N Other'.

The larger model railway manufacturers are articularly good at letting you use their images asked nicely, as it's good publicity for them.

Black and white or colour? Or maybe a ompromise of colour printing on the outer over and black and white inside? Whichever hoice you make will affect the cost, far more in ct than the quantity you order. Very roughly a ll colour newsletter will cost twice the price of black and white one.

If you have a favourite local printer then use em, they'll nearly always be glad of the extra ork. If not, most busy high streets have 'instant rint' shops who usually offer a good service for ich jobs. Talk to them, you'll be surprised how elpful most of them can be, offering advice on roduction and guiding you through the maze f different price variations, depending on size, uantity, colour, etc. But do remember they will ant paying when you collect the job. A lot of ocal printers will open up an account if you ecome a regular customer, usually giving you round 30 days credit. One other increasingly opular and economic source of printing is nding an on-line printer who will accept your ob *via* their website and courier the printed opies back to you a few days later. These often uge printing companies offer some very cheap eals, but you have to know what you're doing nd don't expect much help, like you'd receive rom your local printer.

There is one other cost that must always e considered, that of envelopes, labels and ostage. As I mentioned earlier, an average sized A5 newsletter placed in a C5 sized envelope is quite a bit cheaper to post than an A4 equivalent.

Content
Hopefully your membership will send you articles and photographs to use. I received almost all of the material I used by email, which is great, as the articles don't need to be re-typed nor the photographs scanned.

The actual articles can vary enormously, both in interest and the quality of the writing, so you have to use your judgement as to what to 'edit'. If you can't quite fit it all in then sometimes you need to cut a sentence or two and in most cases you will need to pick up on the odd spelling mistake. I try not to alter the grammar too much unless there is a real howler.

Images sent in can also be extremely variable, but with so many people now owning digital cameras this is proving less of a problem. Occasionally I am sent a poor quality colour print to scan-in, which you can sometimes enhance a little on the computer, but often as not it's best left out. Beware here if members have sent you scanned-in images they have taken from a book or magazine. Again copyright laws are almost certainly being broken, so don't use them unless the permission of the owner of the photograph has been obtained.

Keeping a good supply of articles coming in can also be a problem. However, the better your newsletter looks the more likely your members are to submit articles to you.

We have quite a lively letters page and I encourage members to send me articles on both prototype railways, model railways and anything else to do with our hobby.

When they do send you in an article for publication, always knock out a quick reply acknowledging receipt of the article thanking them for their much-appreciated effort. If they feel valued they are more likely to send in other articles in the future, and thus it rolls on. Finally do get someone else to 'proof-read' the finished document before it goes to the printers. Electronic spell checking is a great asset but incorrect words will still slip through if you're not careful and you'll be surprised just how many mistakes a good second pair of eyes can spot.

The page layout
As I mentioned previously I like the versatility that A4 size gives. I use a combination of one, two or three columns. With A5 only one or two columns is practical. I also like to work within a pre-defined 'template', which makes the whole design consistent and tidy. So although I may have the main text running over three columns I often have an introductory paragraph (with slightly larger or bolder text) run over two and photographs over one, two or three. As a rule of thumb avoid having text columns too wide. It's generally acknowledged that about eight words per line provides the maximum legibility.

I recently saw a newsletter where obviously the editor hadn't been given enough material to fill a particular page. Instead of enlarging

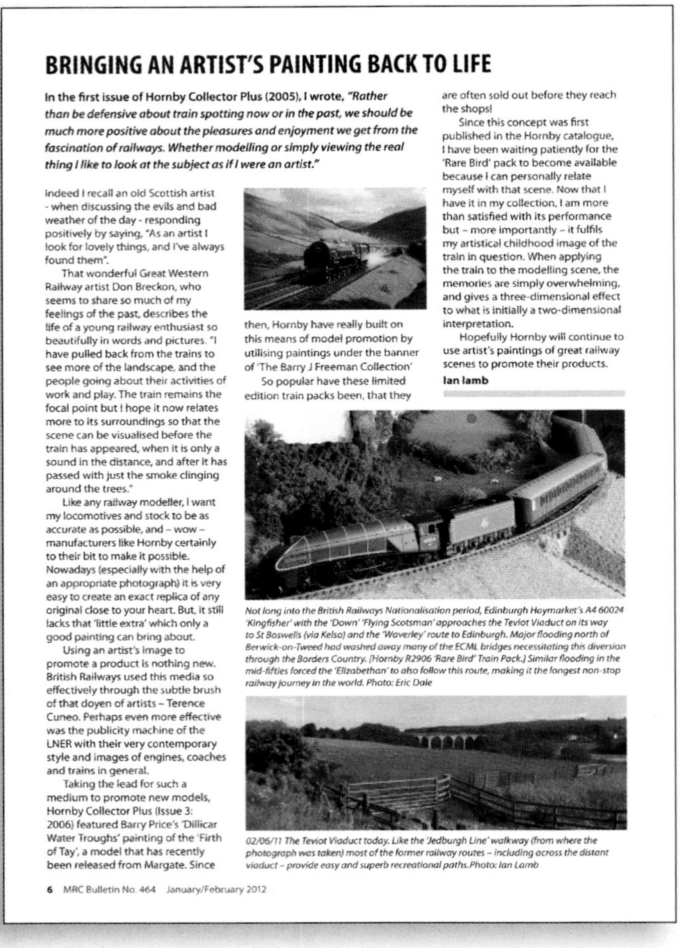

BRINGING AN ARTIST'S PAINTING BACK TO LIFE

In the first issue of Hornby Collector Plus (2005), I wrote, *"Rather than be defensive about train spotting now or in the past, we should be much more positive about the pleasures and enjoyment we get from the fascination of railways. Whether modelling or simply viewing the real thing I like to look at the subject as if I were an artist."*

Indeed I recall an old Scottish artist - when discussing the evils and bad weather of the day - responding positively by saying, "As an artist I look for lovely things, and I've always found them".

That wonderful Great Western Railway artist Don Breckon, who seems to share so much of my feelings of the past, describes the life of a young railway enthusiast so beautifully in words and pictures. "I have pulled back from the trains to see more of the landscape, and the people going about their activities of work and play. The train remains the focal point but I hope it now relates more to its surroundings so that the scene can be visualised before the train has appeared, when it is only a sound in the distance, and after it has passed with just the smoke clinging around the trees."

Like any railway modeller, I want my locomotives and stock to be as accurate as possible, and – wow – manufacturers like Hornby certainly to their bit to make it possible. Nowadays (especially with the help of an appropriate photograph) it is very easy to create an exact replica of any original close to your heart. But, it still lacks that 'little extra' which only a good painting can bring about.

Using an artist's image to promote a product is nothing new. British Railways used this media so effectively through the subtle brush of that doyen of artists – Terence Cuneo. Perhaps even more effective was the publicity machine of the LNER with their very contemporary style and images of engines, coaches and trains in general.

Taking the lead for such a medium to promote new models, Hornby Collector Plus (Issue 3: 2006) featured Barry Price's 'Dillicar Water Troughs' painting of the 'Firth of Tay', a model that has recently been released from Margate. Since then, Hornby have really built on this means of model promotion by utilising paintings under the banner of 'The Barry J Freeman Collection'

So popular have these limited edition train packs been, that they are often sold out before they reach the shops!

Since this concept was first published in the Hornby catalogue, I have been waiting patiently for the 'Rare Bird' pack to become available because I can personally relate myself with that scene. Now that I have it in my collection, I am more than satisfied with its performance but – more importantly – it fulfils my artistical childhood image of the train in question. When applying the train to the modelling scene, the memories are simply overwhelming, and gives a three-dimensional effect to what is initially a two-dimensional interpretation.

Hopefully Hornby will continue to use artist's paintings of great railway scenes to promote their products.

Ian lamb

Not long into the British Railways Nationalisation period, Edinburgh Haymarket's A4 60024 'Kingfisher' with the 'Down' 'Flying Scotsman' approaches the Teviot Viaduct on its way to St Boswells (via Kelso) and the 'Waverley' route to Edinburgh. Major flooding north of Berwick-on-Tweed had washed away many of the ECML bridges necessitating this diversion through the Borders Country. [Hornby R2906 'Rare Bird' Train Pack.] Similar flooding in the mid-fifties forced the 'Elizabethan' to also follow this route, making it the longest non-stop railway journey in the world. Photo: Eric Dale

02/06/11 The Teviot Viaduct today. Like the 'Jedburgh Line' walkway (from where the photograph was taken) most of the former railway routes – including across the distant viaduct – provide easy and superb recreational paths. Photo: Ian Lamb

6 MRC Bulletin No. 464 January/February 2012

IMPROVING THE LINING ON A J52

I own a couple of J52's by Hornby. My engines are in GNR livery which is quite complex and I have always admired the detailed lettering and livery on the models which is way beyond my capabilities.

However, the Hornby model has a black roof which is not exactly correct. I suppose this was due to the limitations of the paint robot. The prototype engines were originally green overall and the lining continued over the roof area.

I decided to investigate how I could complete the painting and lining detail over the roof area of the engine.

The paint used by Hornby is a very close match to 'LNER Doncaster Green' by 'Railmatch'. I painted the black area on the roofs of my two engines using the Railmatch paint. To my eye the colour is identical.

The lining is black with white edging. There may well be alternate ways of achieving this effect. However I remembered some ideas passed on by other modellers. Firstly I drew a dense black line on a sheet of strong white paper, giving a good margin of material on either side. I used a 'UNI Posca ultra fine paint pen' and white A4 paper of the sort one uses in a desktop printer. Other brands of pen may also do the job, but I like UNI pens because they are genuine 'paint pens' as opposed to markers. The 'high tech' solution would be to use a printer to print the lines. Inkjet ink is not permanent and will bleed if dampened. However it may well be possible to achieve similar or better results using a different type of printer.

The next procedure is to cut out the lining strip. To do this I used a new blade in a craft knife and a steel rule to guide the knife while cutting. Safety first - please use a cutting mat in a well lit, uncluttered area. Use a light cutting action to avoid distorting the material and to prevent inadvertent slips while cutting the paper. The material is inexpensive so there is plenty of opportunity to practice.

1. With the steel rule resting on the excess area, the excess white paper is removed by carefully slicing the paper near the black line.
2. Secondly, with the steel rule resting on the excess area, the black line together with a thin white edging is sliced away. The result is a thin strip which is black in the middle and has thin white edges.

If the lining strip is not quite right, it is easy to repeat the process until a satisfactory result is achieved. After trimming to length, slightly overlapping the existing livery, the lining strips were painted with white glue and then glued to the roof and matched to the existing lining.

Tadeusz Opyrchal

One of my engines after treatment

MRC Bulletin No. 464 January/February 2012 5

Here the advantage of using a three-column format is apparent, with headings and intro text going over two columns and images fitting their most suitable width. These of course, can be enlarged, reduced or cropped if it helps fit the article into a required space, though avoid enlarging images that are of poor quality.

the photograph to fill the space, or adding in a small notice about a forthcoming event etc, they just enlarged the text to a huge size to fill the space. It looked awful – don't do it!

I like to see a caption to most pictures, which I usually set one point size smaller and in italics to differentiate from the main text. Surprisingly some modelling magazines don't always use captions so you have to hunt through the text in the hope you're going to find out what the picture is all about.

When producing your newsletter you will inevitably be left with a gap to fill from time to time. Apart from enlarging photos to take up space I have a collection of little panels to use as fillers. These range from announcing 'The next copy date'; 'Don't leave valuables in your car when parked outside the club house'; 'Forthcoming events'; etc. Or maybe you could mention a local exhibition you know about, which would be of interest to your members and which the organisers would be grateful for. Mutual back scratching – they might then give publicity to one of your events (if you let them know!)

The web

We chose to print the 12 pages (sometimes 16) A4 document in black and white to save on costs. But on my computer the 'artwork' is produced in colour, so once the printer has been given a high-resolution PDF converted to black and white to print from, I make a second lower resolution colour PDF. This gets uploaded onto the MRC website (at www.themodelrailwayclub.org) for members and non-members to download if they wish. Back issues are also available, which can be a good source of information if there was an article that someone needs to refer back to. We don't mind non-members downloading copies for their own use, as we consider it's all good publicity for the Club, and that's a very important part of what a good newsletter is all about.

Hopefully you'll enjoy producing your newsletter. I was at the helm of the *Bulletin* for about eight years or so but in that time I've received some wonderful letters of praise, which has made it all seem worthwhile. Mind you, I did get an email once telling me I'd got an apostrophe in the wrong place, so there's no pleasing everyone! **BRM**

THE EDITOR GETS DIRTY… AGAIN!

This is several stories in one… so bear with me.

All set up in my new conservatory! Bill Water's M7 mentioned in the article gets the air brush treatment with my new compressor and airbrush. Note the use of disposable gloves, this helps avoid finger marks on the model. Also, right there in front of me is a photograph of the prototype – something that is a must. I don't yet have an air extractor, so yes… the end doors and windows are open! Photo: ***Glynis Coasby***

It all started many, many years ago…

I suppose of all the model railways skills I may, or may not have, weathering rolling stock is probably my best and certainly the one I get the most enjoyment and satisfaction from.

Although I'm now rapidly approaching retirement age (that is if anyone can afford to 'retire' these days) I have been dabbing paint and gunge on my models ever since my first layout at the age of 13. I remember all those years ago looking at pristine Hornby or Triang locos and thinking somehow there was something about them that just didn't look real.

About the same time, in the early 1960's, I was an avid train spotter and most of what I saw on British Railways were locos and stock that was frequently grimy and run down. But I accepted this as the norm and didn't even give it a second thought.

But then I realised that was the 'secret' – the look of the 00 models I was buying at the time were far too clean. So I started experimenting. I didn't want to completely lose the original paint job but somehow wanted to add some 'dirt'. Luckily I hit on an idea that has become commonplace over the years, but at the time I wasn't aware of anyone else 'ruining' their lovely and pristine models like I was about to. Basically I dabbed them all over with some White Spirit with just a tiny amount of Humbrol Matt Black added in and let the 'dirt' run into all the cracks then let it dry. That was it. Just Matt Black and White Spirit; no other colours; no other techniques. For me at the time it did the trick. My models began to look more realistic.

But the dirtying up of my models never evolved beyond that primitive early stage. Girl friends, marriage and family took priority and model railways were put on the back burner.

Many years later I started back in 00 gauge and again experimented with the overall finish of my models, developing further techniques and learning from other like-minded modellers.

It was my move to O gauge in the 1980's that really focused my desire to investigate all possibilities available to achieve the ultimate look and realism to my stock. My basic technique from all those years ago remained, however I used more colours and once the model was dry I'd use an almost dry brush to add in highlights. Later still I also began to use weathering powders when they were introduced and got some great results. By then I was also admiring some of the airbrushing done on some models seen in the model railway press and decided this had to be my next move.

Luckily, about ten years ago, I was given an ancient compressor from a commercial artist who was retiring, and an even older airbrush. But both worked OK and over the years I'd use all the techniques I had learned, including airbrushing, to get what I considered to be a good result on my models.

I also read a great deal about what other modellers were doing and how they did it. Some were good – some brilliant; but some I considered their weathering was excessive. Probably the most important thing I ever learned was 'paint' what you see, not what you think you see. Always have a photo of the prototype in front of you whenever possible (or a similar prototype), and know when to stop!

I rarely finish a model in one session. It's best to do the main work then set it aside to dry. Remember colours change once they dry. Also, as I mentioned before, it's so easy to overdo it, though this can usually be wiped off at the time if it occurs. Even doing this can sometimes result in some good effects.

However I don't want this to turn into an A, B, C article on how to weather a model. There are plenty of good articles in magazines and books out there if you want to find out more (check out the MRC library). The thing is don't be afraid to experiment. Don't start on an expensive loco, try an old truck first or even some scrap plastic or card.

I mentioned earlier my using an old airbrush and gradually building up my skills. Eventually this faithfull old beast died and at first I tried to continue weathering without it, but realised how much it had become such an important part of my 'tool kit' so somehow or other I had to replace it.

MRC Bulletin No. 464 January/February 2012 7

As mentioned in the main article it's important to use a clear and legible font (typeface). Many clubs and societies have members who are not as young as they once were and find reading small text difficult. For the main text I use 10pt size with 9pt italic for captions.

The benefits of going DIGITAL

BRITISH RAILWAY MODELLING DIGITAL EDITION

Reading *BRM* as a Digital Edition brings with it a mass of benefits to make your favourite railway modelling magazine even better. Here's why you should check out *BRM* as a Digital Edition.

Like it or not, we're in a digital age with computers, tablets and smartphones radically changing the way we interact with the world. There was a time when the very thought of reading a magazine on a computer would have been laughed at, but now it's a growing trend with many magazine readers seeing the benefits of consuming their chosen titles as a Digital Edition. If you haven't enjoyed the benefits of *British Railway Modelling* as a Digital Edition, here's what you're missing:

1 EXTRA PICTURES

The Digital Edition of *BRM* features additional 'Picture Galleries' which include images not shown in the magazine. These galleries are shown by small dot icons at the bottom of an image. Simply click or swipe the images and you'll see the image replaced with a new picture.

2 LIVE WEBSITE LINKS

You'll notice throughout the pages of *BRM* that we link articles in print to additional, free content on either Model-Railways-Live.co.uk or RMweb.co.uk – this could be extra content, bonus images, video or links to forums. Rather than type in the website address and search for the content, readers of the Digital Edition only have to click on the link to be taken to the relevant web page.

3 SAVE MONEY!

You can download the Digital Edition from just £2.49 an issue, that's a saving of £1.26 over the price of the printed magazine. Prices are just:

-month rolling subscription: £2.49 per month
SAVING YOU £1.26
Single issue: £2.99
SAVING YOU 76P
6-month subscription: £13.99
SAVING YOU £8.51
12-month subscription: £26.99
SAVING YOU £18.01

4 NO STORAGE PROBLEMS

Admit it, you've got a batch of magazines stored somewhere (probably gathering dust) and it's getting bigger by the month. By changing to Digital Editions, all future issues will be stored on your computer or tablet device. No more falling over piles of magazines!

5 IMAGE QUALITY

We pride ourselves on producing the best possible model railway layout photography and have recently invested in better quality paper to ensure the image reproduction is vastly improved. However, when you view the images on a computer or tablet you'll appreciate just how much better many of the images really are!

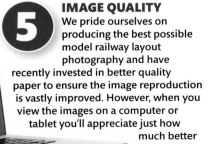

6 ZOOM FUNCTION

Reading a magazine on a computer or tablet allows you to zoom into text or images. This is great news if your eyesight isn't what it once was, or you want to appreciates minute detail in an image.

For more information and to watch our promotional video, go to:
www.model-railways-live.co.uk and click on the Digital Editions icon.

Gresley's first tank loco

William Ascough (Gresley Society and LNER Study Circle) profiles the GNR and LNER J50 Class 0-6-0T. *Photography as credited.*

The Great Northern Railway possessed a series of saddle tank engines for shunting duties which had been first introduced by Patrick Stirling and developed by H A Ivatt. However, an engine with greater adhesion was needed for the steeply graded tracks in the West Riding of Yorkshire so, when Herbert Nigel Gresley became Chief Mechanical Engineer and found himself responsible for the motive power of the GNR he set his mind to the task. The GNR was using Stirling and Ivatt 0-6-0 tender engines for the work radiating from Leeds and Bradford which involved short trips between stations, sidings and collieries, shunting as necessary to pick-up or set-down along the way. The new design for this work produced in 1914 was a large innovative 0-6-0 tank engine. The design used reconditioned boilers recovered from withdrawn locomotives and large side tanks. The tank tops were sloped down at the front

in order to give the footplate crews a clear view of the line ahead. Further, a large aperture for access purposes was provided in the tank sides behind the cylinders to allow for oiling the inside valve gear and slidebars of the new engines.

General design

The first ten engines of this new design were brought out in 1914 and given the Nos.157-164/6/7. Apart from the design features detailed above these ten engines had a relatively short bunker and long side tanks extending right to the front of the smokebox. The reconditioned boilers used on these ten engines were 4' 2" diameter recovered from Ivatt 0-8-2 tanks which were then being withdrawn from service.

These boilers had extra long fireboxes which extenuated the proportions of the new design which was classified class J23 by the GNR. Using

recovered boilers of the same type a further 20 engines appeared from Doncaster Works between 1914 and 1919 and given Nos.168-176/8 and 211-20. The design for these engines used 5½" shorter tanks whereas the boilers were the same length as before and thus extended in front of the tanks on waisted saddles taken down to the footplate. These engines were also extended at the rear to accommodate longer bunkers which were of the usual open rectangular type and had simple hinged ventilators in their cab roof. One of these engines, No.175, was notable with the dome seen to be much further back than usual as it carried a boiler from a Stirling single engine! A further ten engines were built by the GNR numbered 221-30. The reconditioned boilers used on these engines were 4' 5" diameter – this time recovered from tender engines being withdrawn from service. These engines had the shorter tanks and longer bunkers.

At the front the smokebox was just in front of the tanks but the saddle was further back allowing the front of the frames to be seen extending to the front bufferbeam. The GNR classified all these engines as class J23, however, at the grouping when the LNER was formed they were re-classified into classes J51 (engines with the smaller boilers) and J50, the engines with the larger boilers. In 1923 a further ten engines Nos.3231-40 were being built to this modified J50 type which was then adopted by the LNER as the Group Standard design for shunting engines.

In service development by the LNER

In service the weight distribution of the first engines Nos.157-164/6/7, was found to need some alteration. This was achieved by blanking off the front end of the side tanks. To compensate for the loss of water capacity a further water tank was fitted below the bottom of the coal bunker. The top of this tank formed the bottom of the bunker and so it was sloped forward to a shovelling plate. However, this design feature restricted the very limited coal capacity in the bunker. To enhance this coal capacity a self trimming grillage cage was added to the top of the open bunker which gave these engines a unique appearance. The grillage was cut away to allow a rear view for the crew by blanking off the inner part of the rear spectacles.

As detailed the design was adopted by the LNER for the future and further engines of the J50 class were ordered and built from 1926 when a batch of 38 new engines appeared for use throughout the system including Scotland.

In this batch the roof was modified to a gentler radius to conform to the composite rolling stock gauge. These engines were classified J50/3 and were not fitted with the vacuum brake. They were numbered 583/6

/8/9/91/3/4/6/601/3/9/10/6-8/21/2/35/6/ 1037/41/5/58/63/8-70/4/9/81/2/6 and 2789-94. The engines had the open rectangular bunkers and those which were to work in Scotland were fitted with NBR shunters' footsteps and handrails. Other features were balanced wheels, under footplate injectors, raised tank fillers, Ross Pop safety valves, improved cab ventilators and left-hand drive. They also had plain rather than fluted coupling rods and from No.1037 (later 8959) Group Standard double shouldered buffers rather than the GN type.

Boiler development and rebuilding

The first 30 engines forming class J51 started out with smaller boilers than the later engines which formed class J50. The tank front was flush with the front of the smokebox on the original ten engines, Nos.3157-64/6/7 (later Nos. 8890-9) whereas on the next 20 the tanks were shortened to expose the smokebox front - Nos.3168-78, 3211-20 (later 8900-19). In the case of the next ten engines with the larger boilers the tank sides were no longer flush across the engine - Nos.3221-30 (later 8920-9). These larger boilers were shorter than those previously used.

Another difference was that the smokebox wrapper had a cylindrical form with the valve chest cover recessed under the smokebox. The front frames on these ten J50/2 and all the following J50/3 and J50/4 engines projected above the footplate and extended as far as the bufferbeam. Starting in 1929 all the earlier engines were reboilered to form classes J50/1 and J50/2. This work was completed in 1935 when class J51 became extinct, however, the rebuilds retained their original valve chest cover so that the front was flush with the front of their side tanks.

J50/1 No.3161 in front of J50/2 No.3217 shows the comparison between the original GNR cab and the LNER one. This engine has a short bunker and a flush front with the steps on the front of the tanks. Vacuum brake fitted. *Les Perkins/ FA Wycherley*

Detail differences

In addition to the J50/4 engines detailed above, all the early engines of classes J50/1 and J50/2 were fitted with the vacuum brake. The engines of type J50/3 had steam brakes.

After the first ten engines with short bunkers had been tried in service there was found a need to increase coal capacity. The length of all the following engines was increased by 16" at the rear end to make them 4' 2" long with a capacity of 3 ½ tons. The back of the bunker was no longer recessed behind a wooden beam but brought level with the face of the bufferbeam. The extended bunkers were rectangular in plan with coal rails at the top and the coal rails were all fitted with backing plates to control spillage by 1931. Of the final batch of engines to be built, the J50/4 group, Nos.584/5/7/90/5/5/8/9, 600/2/5/6/8/11/5, (later Nos.8978-91) were fitted with a built-up hopper type bunker sloping on either side of modified rear windows thereby increasing the coal capacity to five tons five hundredweight. This last batch also had vacuum brakes and steam heating pipes for Empty Coaching Stock workings.

The first ten GN engines had sandwich type timber bufferbeams which were eventually replaced with 1" thick steel plates, becoming standard for the class.

J50/1 No.68892 showing detail of short bunker with coal rails and as running in BR days. This engine now has a screw coupling and AWS gear fitted. It also seems to have a short dome fitted. *R K Blencowe*

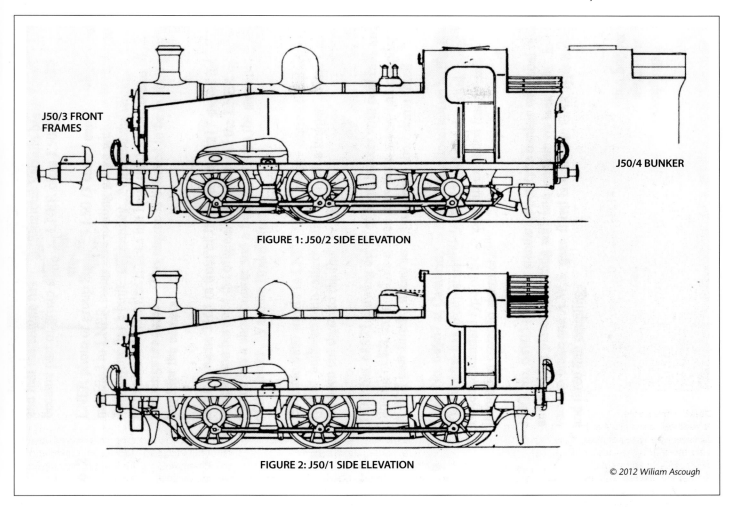

J50/3 FRONT FRAMES

J50/4 BUNKER

FIGURE 1: J50/2 SIDE ELEVATION

FIGURE 2: J50/1 SIDE ELEVATION

© 2012 Wiliam Ascough

The class was normally fitted with the Doncaster 2' 7" built-up chimney. Engines Nos.3222-30 were initially fitted with a wide tapering design. One of these chimneys was also fitted to No.3169 for a time. All the engines with tapering chimneys later had them replaced with the built-up type.

Engines allocated to Scotland, Nos.616-8/21/2/35/6 (later 8952-8) had plain coupling rods as did those with numbers starting with 1000 and 2789 (later 8959-72).

Several J50s had grab irons on the smokebox set at an angle rather than straight as was more usual.

As set out above the first ten engines with short bunkers, Nos.157-64/6/7 (later 8890-9) were fitted with cage type hopper bunkers built-up from coal rails – as was engine No.173 for a short time only. On these engines the rear windows were partly plated in to prevent damage from lumps of coal. The final batch of engines to be built – the J50/4 group Nos.584/5/7/90/5/5/8/9, 600/2/5/6/8/11/5 (later Nos.8978-91), were fitted with a built-up hopper type bunker sloping on either side of modified rear windows thereby increasing the coal capacity to five tons five hundredweight. This last batch also had vacuum brakes and steam heating pipes for ECS workings.

The GNR fitted engine No.167 with a Robinson superheater and a boiler which operated at 175psi. This did not show any significant advantage over the other engines and so it remained a one-off until 1930 when as No.3167 the engine was rebuilt as a J50/1. This engine was also fitted with a Wakefield

No.7 six-feed mechanical lubricator mounted on the right-hand side of the footplate behind the leading splasher.

The original ten engines (Nos.8890-9) did not have roof ventilators fitted. The following engines (8900-39) were fitted with a simple hinged plate to allow for some cab ventilation. The group standard engines (J50/3 and J50/4) were all fitted with improved ventilators which

allowed these engines to work across London to the Southern Railway.

All the sandboxes were below the footplate, in the case of the first 20 GNR engines the front sandboxes were placed in advance of the leading wheels. These engines had funnels for filling the sandboxes fitted well above the footplate level on the front of the engine. Subsequent engines had the sandboxes located

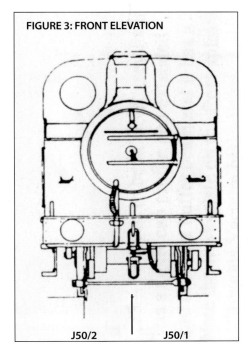

FIGURE 3: FRONT ELEVATION

J50/2   J50/1

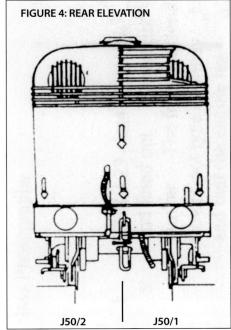

FIGURE 4: REAR ELEVATION

J50/2   J50/1

J50/3 No.68967 at Cambridge - note shed allocation on buffer beam. This engine has group standard buffers fitted and three link couplings. Note builders plate on tank side at front, no vacuum pipes, and standard type of front end with extended frames and inspection cover to steam chest. *L R Peters*

further back to provide sand ahead of the central driving wheels located behind the footsteps. The fillers were found in the tank side recess. All of the class was then modified to this arrangement.

The engines which worked in Scotland (616-8/21/2/35/6) were all fitted with additional steps below the bunker extending from the cab footsteps to the rear bufferbeam. These engines also had drop-grates fitted.

As engines were reallocated to London in 1952 it became necessary for gauging purposes and starting with No.68965 to reduce the overall width over the footsteps from 8' 8" to

8' 6". This was to enable these engines to work across London to the Southern Region.

The original GNR engines were fitted with Ramsbottom type safety valves and their whistle was mounted in front of the cab – but with its tip slightly above roof level. The group standard engines, J50/3 and J50/4 (later Nos 8940-91) were all fitted with plain Ross pop safety valves.

The GNR engines had Doncaster worksplates fitted to the leading splasher under the tanks and were originally painted in Slate Grey lined out in white. The numbers and letters were also white shaded black. After the 1914-18 war

Nos.221-30 the first J50 engines were finished with a more ornate lining having scalloped corners. At Grouping the livery for the whole class was specified as black lined out with red and 3,000 was added to all loco numbers.

The new Group standard J50/3s had works plates fitted to the tanksides at the front. After 1928 the red lining was left off and during the 1939-45 war the lettering was simplified to 'NE' only. In 1944 engine No.2789 was temporarily painted grey on one side with the No.8900 so that the class could be included in a report on standard designs for future years. In 1945 the first ten engines were renumbered

J50/2 No. 68905 showing standard open type bunker with coal rails and backing plates as running with late emblem on tank side. It has vacuum brake and AWS gear fitted but still has GNR type buffers and three link couplings. *R K Blencowe*

J50/1 No.8891 still in LNER lined green, fitted with a short bunker built-up with rails into the form of a hopper. Note cab roof cut down to the flatter radius andbuiders plate on on leading splasher.. *A C W Carraway*

as Nos.3180-9, whilst in 1946 the whole class was renumbered Nos.8890-8991 in order of cnstruction. During the same year one engine, J50/1No.8891, was turned out in LNER green with gold shaded numbers and lettering. However, this remained a solitary example. The whole class entered BR stock with 60,000 added to their numbers. Departmental engines Nos.10-6 (68911/4/7/28/61/71/6) were used at Doncaster in various workshops there.

Allocations
The GNR engines were sent to the Leeds/ Bradford district and became known as the 'Ardsley' tanks for shunting and local trip goods trains. After Grouping, No.3238 was sent to Edinburgh, No.3239 to Sheffield, 3240

to Immimgham, 3221 to Peterborough and 3222 to Nottingham for trials. Despite these trials, most of the new J50/3s went to Leeds. Then Nos.616-8/21/2/35/6 (8952-8) were allocated to Eastfield shed in Glasgow. Of these Nos.8952/7 in 1946 were found at St Margarets in Edinburgh whilst in 1957 Nos.68953/7 went to Polmadie! No.1058 went to March shed and No.1074 was tried out at Whitemoor yard. New engines Nos.2789-93 went to Immingham, and Stratford in East London was sent Nos.1069/74 and 2794 (8965/7/77) for working Goodmayes and other yards. The class was also found at Frodingham, Leicester, Tuxford and Woodford.

The allocation of the J50/4s with the hopper bunkers was widespread with new engines also working from Annesley, Colwick, Doncaster,

Hitchin and Hornsey with No.615 at Norwich and Nos.600/2 at Cambridge. the arrival of engines at the southern end of the line thus began in 1938, although these were transferred away during wartime, only to return in 1952 when 30 engines were transferred there for shunting, empty coach working and transfer trips to the SR and other Regions.

Models
In OO, an early cast metal kit produced by K's fitted the Hornby-Dublo R1 chassis, while Lima produced a model with a very basic chassis which didn't have coupling pins on the centre driving wheels. A photo-etched kit is available from Ace Products in 4mm, 7mm and gauge 1 which builds into any variation of the class. BRM

J50/4 No.68991 showing the extended bunker fitted with a hopper almost to the top of the cab. Note the small rear view window and the two steps on the bunker side. Fitted with screw couplings, vacuum brake and group standard buffers. *R K Blencowe*

Network Rail New Measurement Train

Modelling the 'Doctor Banana' yellow HST in N gauge by **Nigel Burkin**.

Photography by the author.

A smart looking HST book set by Dapol provides the basis for modelling the Network Rail New Measurement Train.

A twin HST power car book set released by Dapol in early 2012 is the driver behind this project to build a complete Network Rail 'New Measurement Train' (NMT) for operation on the *BRM* N gauge project layout Dudley Heath. Formed from various Mk.3 trailers of various vintages in 2003 (together with a Mk.2f), its shorter formation compared to a regular service HST is the attraction: currently five trailers plus two power cars as opposed to seven trailers and power cars for a Cross Country set means a potentially better fit to the layout. Over-long trains can overwhelm the restricted dimensions of the layout and cause problems in the fiddle yard. In the event, the NMT model only just fits the layout and in some areas, it's a squeeze!

Dapol's book set provided the motive power for the project: surrogate HST DVT type power car No. 43 014 together with a model of 43 062 with its full fairing, both finished in Network Rail colours. All that is needed to complete the train are the five trailers regularly used in the NMT from around 2007 following various attempts to incorporate a Mk.2f High Speed Recording Coach into the formation modified for 125mph operation. In the event, the Mk.2f did not have the braking capability for speeds of more than 110mph resulting in its withdrawal from the NMT formation.

My time stamp for the project is circa 2009-10 when I observed and photographed the train with five trailers on several occasions. Other trailers have been used in the past, including hybrid power battery car No. 977996 in experiments to develop hybrid power technology and the occasional use of the reserve generator vehicle No. 977995.

975984

Former prototype Mk.3 buffet car, No. W40000 is one of the former Railway Technical Centre vehicles now used in the NMT. In the past, it was Laboratory 15 'Argus' used for data collection during testing in the field. The coach is now used as a staff coach and generator car.

977994

Track Recording Trailer No.977994 is a

Power car 43 014 is one of the pool of three used on the NMT, Nos.43 013 and 43 062 being the other traction available for the train. It was a surrogate DVT for push-pull testing before reverting back to regular use as an HST power car and retains its front drawgear.

Trailer No.975984 is one of the two prototype HST trailers adapted for use as a staff and generator car in the NMT. Originally numbered W40000, it was a buffet car in the prototype HST set and later as Laboratory 15, *Argus*.

977994 is a former Trailer Guard's Second (TGS) trailer numbered 44087, fitted out as a track recording coach.

Pantograph fitted 977993 is the most complex coach in the set to model and is an OHLE data recording coach. Formerly TGS No. 44053, it was once in revenue service but made surplus through train re-formations.

former (TGS) Trailer Guards Standard vehicle No.44087 fitted out with sensors to monitor rail condition, the equipment for which can be seen on the right-hand bogie in front of the inner wheel set. The bodyshell is similar to that of No.977993, a note modellers should make when modelling the NMT. The roof has little or no additional equipment and is the simplest to represent in model form.

977993

By far the most challenging trailer to model is the Over Head Line Equipment (OHLE) data recording coach which is rebuilt former TGS No.44053. Whilst the body is simply converted using the etched window frames provided in the PH Designs kit, the roof is another matter, requiring a pantograph well, modified Dapol pantograph and other roof equipment.

975814

A simple trailer to model compared to the OHLE test coach is prototype HST trailer No.41000, used previously as Test Car 10, an instrument coach for high speed testing but now a conference trailer in the NMT. It has no raised window frames, so etched ones are not provided for it in the conversion kit, and has several windows plated over on one

side making it a simple vehicle to model. The hardest part is changing the roof to represent a Mk.3a loco hauled type with the small vents at each end; a feature of the prototype HST trailers. Modifications to the Dapol coach roof moulding mean that ribs matching the moulded ones have to be added to each end. A simple method is to use the strands from stripped 7/0.2 copper wire.

977984

The last coach in a typical formation and coupled to the opposite power car, former TRFK HST catering trailer No. 40501 is used as a staff and generator trailer. Roof detail is similar to a TRFK catering trailer but with modified panels at each end. It is modelled using etched window frames and grilles. Several windows are wholly or partially blanked out with special

The second prototype HST trailer used in the NMT is 975814, formerly No.41000 which was taken into departmental use as Test Car 10.

Former HST catering car (TRFK) 40501 is adapted as a staff coach and numbered 977984.

Above: One power car represents No.43 062 with unmodified front fairing. This is the non-motorised power car of the Dapol book set.

Right: The second power car offered in the Dapol book set is 43 014, a former surrogate HST DVT with buffer beam and buffers. The model is supplied with air brake pipes to fit to the buffer beam which should be red in colour.

Below: Hornby also offers its HST power car models in OO gauge together with a train pack of two trailers used in the NMT.

inserts supplied in the kit and finished with filler.

Modelling options

There are two options for modelling the NMT in its 2009 guise: Vinyl overlays (by Electra Railway Graphics) applied to Graham Farish Mk.3 coaches, completed by partially repainting and converting the roof mouldings. Alternatively, conversion enthusiasts may wish to try the new conversion kit by PH Designs designed to convert newer and better Dapol Mk.3 models.

The former method relies on the removal of printed sides from the transparent body shells of Graham Farish Mk.3 coaches and applying self-adhesive vinyl overlays which are printed with all of the required livery details. Window openings are pre-cut in the correct positions to complete the conversion and grilles are printed in place. For those wary of repainting and major modelling work, the vinyl overlay route is a pragmatic one which I have successfully used for a number of projects in the past, including three Mk.3 locomotive hauled coaches of the EWS executive train, a project featured the September 2011 issue of *BRM*.

The PH Designs conversion kit is composed of etched window frames and window blanks. The conversion involves removing window frame detail from the Dapol models and applying new ones, whilst blanking out certain windows on all of the coaches and adding etched grilles to two of the five trailers. Repainting and the application of transfers is essential to completing the trailers. It's a more involved route than using pre-coloured overlays. The attraction of this route is in the use of the Dapol models as a basis because they certainly have an edge over the older Graham Farish Mk.3 models with individually fitted flush glazing, better defined moulded detail and better overall proportions.

The project

All but one of the Dapol Mk.3 trailers used as base models are converted using new window frames and various window blanking plates. The

Above: Two manufacturers offer Mk.3 trailers in N gauge - Dapol with its relatively new range which is to be enhanced with RFMs (front), and Graham Farish with its clear-sided version which is over-printed with different window configurations (rear).

Right: One option for modelling the New Measurement Train is to use Electra Railway Graphics vinyl overlays on Graham Farish models. The technique involves minimal painting and results in neatly finished models with flush glazing and all of the relevant markings.

Tools and materials:

- PH Design etchings NMT conversion pack
- Five (six if building the generator car) Dapol Mk.3 trailers
- Dapol Becknell Willis pantograph
- Railtec Models Network Rail lining and logo waterslide transfers
- Needle files
- Pin vice
- Selection of HSS drills from 0.45mm to 1mm diameter
- Grade 1200 wet and dry paper
- Modelling knife and new blades 0.75mm diameter plastic rod
- 20 thou and 40 thou styrene card - small off-cuts are sufficient
- 15 thou x 60 thou styrene strip
- Short length of stripped 7/0.2mm equipment wire
- Typewriter correction fluid used as a fine filler
- 'Squadron White' putty

technique allows the original moulded glazing to be re-used and involves stripping the models to bare body shells, with the glazing carefully removed and set to one side. A fine cut needle file is used to remove all raised detail including window frames between the inner door lines, leaving a smooth finish ready for the application of new window frames.

Each frame and grille was carefully snipped from the etched sheet, noting how the various parts are grouped together by trailer with the vehicle numbers etched on the sheet for easy identification. Examining the frames, note how they have a small lip enabling the modeller to position them in each window opening as straight and level as possible. A steel rule is an important tool for ensuring the window frames are level when viewed along the coach. Thin CA glue is the perfect adhesive, applied sparingly to the frame before application.

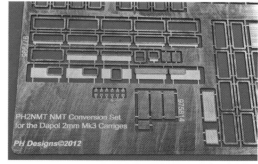

Above: A close up view of the PH Designs etch showing the etched frames with lips for fitting to the Dapol models. The parts for six NMT trailers are included on the etch including one not modelled in this project, reserve generator vehicle No. 977995.

Left: Dapol Mk.3 trailers form the basis of a second route for modelling the NMT in N gauge using a kit composed of etched window frames and grilles produced by PH Designs. It is this second method which has been used to build the NMT described in this article.

The project is a long and involved one, requiring a great deal of careful examination of photographs to correctly position each window frame and grille. It helps to mark the vehicle number on the underside of the roof and body mouldings for easy identification and to work on one vehicle at a time. Each window frame is very thin which means that the modeller has only one chance of getting it right. Removing them after the glue has hardened is likely to damage a frame beyond redemption!

Of the five trailers, only one is not modified with etched window frames: No. 975814. Several windows are plated over on one side of the coach and carefully finished flush with the coach sides. Otherwise, the stripped and filed bodyshell can be carefully finished with wet and dry paper to remove all traces of moulded frames and door lock lights prior to priming and painting.

There is some finishing work to complete before all of the bodyshells enter the painting booth. Traces of excess glue should be removed and the frames very carefully rubbed with a fibre pencil to remove tarnish. It pays to give each bodyshell a final check against photographs of the full size vehicles to be sure all of the frames are correctly positioned. A coat of primer follows which provides the ideal undercoat for livery painting and will reveal any faults in the finishing of the bodyshell.

Roof detail

Roof detail is a tricky area to work on and involves some careful modifications in the case of three of the trailers if a close representation of the full size trailers is desired. Some modellers may be satisfied with simply refitting the roof mouldings after painting whilst others may decide to have a go at the pantograph well of trailer No.977993. The two models representing the prototype trailers were modified to the small end ventilator format by removing the two large blocks from the roof ends, making the three vents located on each end of the trailers from 15 thou x 60 thou styrene strip. Replicating

Dapol Mk.3 trailers are easily dismantled, starting with the roof which is clipped to spigots moulded to the glazing inserts.

Glazing is removed next by working it carefully from the openings. It does not matter if it is broken into several sections provided the roof clips (indicated by red arrows) are undamaged.

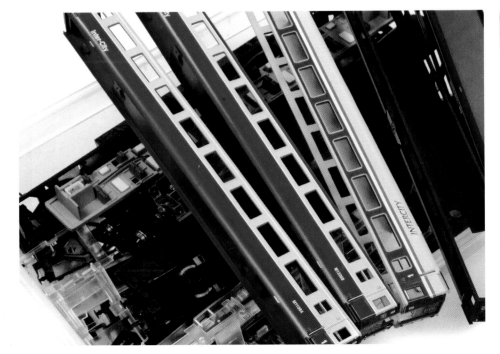

Above: Work commences by removing the moulded window frames from each of the five trailer bodies using a fine cut needle file.

Left: Modelling the usual five-car NMT set is a relatively big undertaking and takes some time. Five dismantled trailers soon fills a storage box with parts that need to be kept safely to one side.

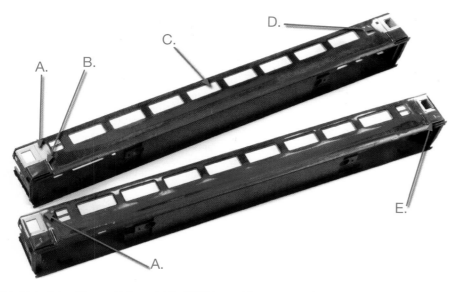

Removal of dividing bars from the toilet compartment windows to model No. 975814.

One trailer body is put to one side to model No. 975814, one of the prototype HST trailers. It has no raised window frames. Stripping of detail should include the door lock lights (A), all moulded frames (C) together with the toilet window frames and dividing bar (D). Detail to keep includes hand rails (B) and foot steps (E).

Each trailer is converted to NMT trailers by first fitting the full size window frames using a tiny quantity of CA glue. A lip on the inside of the etch helps with alignment of the frames.

the roof ribs needed some thought and I eventually came up with the idea of making them with strands from stripped 7/0.2mm equipment wire. Only short lengths were required to finish the roof ends and it worked surprisingly well!

Other details, verified using reference photographs included the various cowls on former catering vehicles and the various roof pods which contain aerials and transponders. The trickiest roof to complete was that of the pantograph fitted trailer. It's length and position was determined from photographs and cut into the roof using a razor saw, the initial hole being smaller than required. A file was used to open up the well to the desired size and a small piece of 20 thou black styrene fitted to make the well floor. 'Squadron' putty was used to both fill and shape the outer end of the well whilst the inner end is flat, formed of a piece of 20 thou black styrene.

The well was equipped with a cut down Dapol 'Brecknell Willis' pantograph model with a little addition of styrene strip and rod to represent insulators and the frame structure. Other roof equipment including the measurement equipment boxes was represented with styrene sheet filed to shape.

With the roof modifications of the trailers complete, they were painted black and weathered using roof dirt colour. The pantograph and associated equipment was picked out in grey before a final light application of weathering.

Livery painting

Fortunately, after such an involved conversion, the painting of the five trailers is straightforward: black roof (except No. 977995 which had a grey roof at the time stamp of the project) and yellow bodyshell with a double blue on white line and Network Rail logos. Underframes and bogies are black, although weathered, as are the coach ends. An orange stripe is applied along the cantrail.

The coat of grey primer applied following completion of the conversion work is the ideal

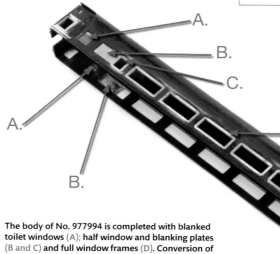

The body of No. 977994 is completed with blanked toilet windows (A); half window and blanking plates (B and C) and full window frames (D). Conversion of No. 977993's bodyshell is similar in style. The roof is another matter!

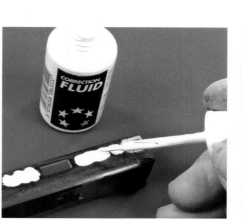

Three window blanks are provided to model No. 975814 which are glued in place and the joins filled with typewriter correction fluid - the perfect fine filler for this type of work.

Part window blanks used in the four trailers fitted with etched frames are treated with type writer correction fluid to fill any tiny gaps and gently rubbed down to a smooth finish.

Once the window frames are all fitted and the blanked off windows rubbed down to a fine finish, the five trailer bodies are primed and sprayed Network Rail yellow.

undercoat for a double application of Network Rail yellow. Two coats give the colour depth and is followed by a coat of gloss varnish to which the lining and Network Rail logo transfers may be applied. The coaches were subsequently varnished with satin varnish and weathered with a single wash of roof dirt colour diluted 20:1 with paint thinners. The same wash was applied to the power car models to tone down the livery and highlight the grille detail. Interestingly enough, the trailers were progressively repainted during 2011 and 2012 without markings resulting in plain yellow vehicles marshalled in the set for a while with only the running number applied, a great way to simplify the project. The trailer roof colour also changed from black to mid grey at the same time.

Fitting the glazing

The conversion kit allows for the re-use of the glazing inserts fitted to the base models. They can all be reused except the toilet compartment window mouldings because the glazing bars have been removed from the trailers. The inserts are checked for unwanted 'no smoking' and 'first class'

Water slide transfers are best applied to a gloss finish to avoid carrier film 'silvering'. The NMT transfers used on the NMT project were produced by Railtec Models.

Transfers are applied, the bodies varnished and the original glazing reinserted, noting the position of the roof clip spigots ensuring the roof mouldings will clip back into place.

The roof of pantograph fitted 977993 is modified by cutting a pantograph well into one end.

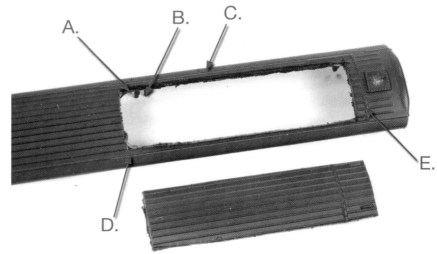

Care is taken to cut the hole within the required area and the roof clips (B) which must be unmodified. The hole is filed out to the required size as indicated by lines (C) and (D) whilst the remains of the hatch detail is pared away (E).

A. B. C.

Phoenix Precision paint colours:
• **Frame dirt (P960)**
• **Dull black (P975)**
• **Dull white (P976)**
• **Network Rail yellow (P310)**
• **Network Rail roof grey (P311)** for some trailers
• **Gloss varnish (PV62)**
• **Satin varnish (PV72)**

The pantograph well is completed by fitting an end piece on the inner end (A); a floor of 20 thou black styrene (B) and filler which will allow the carving to shape of the outer end (C).

Two prototype HST trailers are used in the NMT and both have different roof detail compared to 'production' HST trailers. The roof for 975814 (front) and 975984 (rear) are shown in this picture. Once completed, the roof mouldings were painted black and weathered with roof dirt.

Each of the trailer chassis were ballasted with 40 grams of weight using small pieces of roofing lead. The additional mass will improve performance of the train when propelled.

labels which must be removed with paint solvent before clipping them back into place. Note the position of the roof clips and the corresponding spigots moulded on the glazing if the inserts are being refitted in small pieces. It is important to retain the spigots so the roof mouldings can be reinstated!

The internal seating mouldings were not reused in the trailers and to disguise the lack of an interior, pieces of tinted glazing material were glued to the inside of each coach side.

Weathering and final details
A wash of roof dirt paint to a dilution of 20:1 has already been mentioned. Whilst the paint applied to roof and bodyshell mouldings was drying, the power cars were also treated to frame dirt weathering and a drift of exhaust over the roof.

The buffer beam of No.43 014 was primed with grey general purpose primer and painted red.

Each trailer underframe and bogie moulding was weathered with frame dirt colour before the brake discs were fitted to the wheels and around 40 grams of additional weight was fitted to improve performance. After all, the train will be expected to perform well when being propelled by the motorised power car (No.43 014 of the book set pair) and additional weight will help the trailers to track through curves and junctions.

The final detail was the fitting of Digitrax DZ125IN decoders to the six-pin DCC sockets fitted to both power car models; the one in No.43 062 was needed to operate the lighting circuits. Both models were placed on the programming track at the same time ensuring both decoders picked up the same address.

During the running-in turns on Dudley Heath, it was noted that the leading bogies of both power cars had a tendency to derail when approaching facing turnouts from time to time. This was tracked down to the wheels of the leading bogie rubbing against the underside of the underframe detail moulding. This was modified by removing the offending area of plastic and gluing the front section of the moulding into the front fairing area of the body. The chassis could still be removed for maintenance without difficulty and performance was much enhanced following the modification.

Testing of the train set involves looking for problems and this means running it in both directions, both propelling with the motorised power car to the rear and to the front whilst carefully observing how it runs over junctions and into curves.

Left: Another view of full size NMT power car No.43 062.

Below: Rounding the south curve on Dudley Heath, the project N gauge layout, is power car No. 43 062, leading the NMT on one of its first test runs in preparation for its use at the Peterborough show.

Conclusion

Modelling a complete train rather than one coach or trailer makes for a long and involved project and the modeller has to be aware of past train re-formations, changes to the vehicles themselves to meet changes in testing criteria and of course, changes to the livery following overhauls. The Network Rail NMT is a popular prototype and the perfect test train in model form. Being able to use Dapol models throughout the project thanks to the etched conversion kit by PH Designs makes for a consistent looking train, albeit quite a financial investment in models.

Around 40 hours was needed to complete the project including roof detail. Was it worth it? Well, the model is already a popular addition to the Dudley Heath line-up and the smooth performance of the Dapol HST power cars ensures that it has a regular turn during operating sessions! BRM

Prototype HST trailer, now conference car No. 975814, is finished without raised window frames and fitted with a modified roof in the same manner as the full size trailer.

The most complex vehicle in the set is No. 977993 with its pantograph well and roof equipment.

Project details:
- **Scale:** N (1:148)
- **Conversion complexity (on a scale of 1 to 10):** 7
- **Degree of involvement:** Removal and replacement of significant plastic details, fitting etched details, filling and repainting
- **Conversion time from start to finish:** 40 hours over several weeks plus paint drying time
- **Cost of materials:** £35.00 excluding base coaches and power cars.
- **Base models:** Dapol Mk.3 TSO or FO trailers.

Useful websites:
- www.railtec-models.com
- www.dapol.co.uk
- www.phd-design-etchings.co.uk
- www.departmentals.com

Trailer 977994 with its plain roof and modified window arrangement is the simplest of the etched conversions to complete.

The 'Jinty' reverses into the dock after taking on water at the water tower.

DUTCH RIVER DOCK

Ralph Nuttall's compact 7mm layout, based on the dock workings at Goole. *Photography by the author.*

One of my New Year resolutions in January 1962 was to see and photograph as many of the locomotives still in existence which had been built by the Lancashire & Yorkshire Railway. There was a total of 33 in British Railways stock, comprising ten 0-4-0 saddle tanks, three 0-6-0 saddle tanks, 17 0-6-0 tender locomotives, plus two preserved and one in industrial use. I had seen all of these previously, with the exception of one tender locomotive, three of the 0-4-0 'Pugs', and the 'Pug' employed at Charlton Glass Works, in South East London. I eventually photographed this loco two years later.

The three dock tanks that I had not seen were shedded at Goole, for shunting around the very tight curves in the docks. At a level crossing, I asked the gatekeeper if the 'Pugs' were working. He said they had not worked for

some time and the docks were now shunted by diesels - confirming this information a North British diesel shunter trundled past with a rake of wagons. He said I would probably see them at the shed and gave me instructions to get there walking through the docks. Looking back, it seems amazing in these days of Health & Safety at Work that a young teenager could walk through a busy docks system, without safety clothing, and no one taking any notice. However, on approaching the shed area I walked into the shed foreman, who informed me that it was not possible to see or photograph the 'Pugs' and that I should remove myself from Railway property immediately! As I made my way back to the station I decided I would return later in the month, but never did and the 'Pugs' were cut up. I was resigned never to see steam working at Goole Docks.

Forty one years later, I received a telephone

call one evening from my friend, Geoff Silcock, who informed me that he was arranging a photo-shoot at Goole, with a preserved 'Pug' shunting wagons around what is left of the system. Would I be interested in joining his party? So on March 1, 2003, a gloriously sunny day, cold but ideal for photographing steam locomotives, I was back at Goole Docks, taking photographs of a 'Pug' as it shunted all the remaining sidings. The system is still used and shunted by an 08 diesel, the traffic appears to be mainly steel coil. The overhead railways, used for shunting coal wagons to tipplers that sent the coal into the holds of ships have gone, but the system still retains atmosphere amongst the tight curves and large cranes. One of the coal hoists is preserved, and the water tower and an enginemen's bothy from steam days remains.

At this time I was looking to buy a new car, the one I had was nine years old with over

A view across the yard, with the 'Pug' in the background.

100,000 miles on the clock and starting to show its age. The choice was narrowed down to two makes, so a visit was paid to the showrooms of these dealers, plus visits to internet sites and eventually a new car was purchased. At this time I had an O gauge exhibition layout, Glen Fiddich, which I had built only 18 months previously, which I had plans to develop further. It was booked for an exhibition in Hertfordshire one Saturday and fortunately as it turned out, I decided to load the layout into the new car on the Friday afternoon, rather than the evening. As I was putting it into the car I became aware of a problem, no matter which way round the layout was loaded it just would not fit into the space available. By now it was 5.00pm and there was no way I could transport the layout to the exhibition. What had gone wrong? At both the motor show and the car dealership I had carefully measured the rear of the car to make sure it would take the model railway. Realisation then dawned. I had measured the floor space, forgetting that on most cars the rear slopes inwards, the car rear door was hitting the top of the layout; it was only about an inch too long, but this was a crucial inch.

I telephoned around the local van hire people, but I live in a rural area and there are few of them, none could help. I thought that I was going to make myself very unpopular with an exhibition manager, crying off at about twelve hours notice. Then a thought struck me. Although I had sold my old car, the new owner had not collected it and it was still sitting on my drive. I called my car insurance company at a few minutes to six and was surprised to find someone there, they agreed to re-insure it for 48 hours, although at a very large premium, so Glen

A 2-8-0 'Austerity' comes under the bridge from the hidden sidings.

An ex-Lancashire & Yorkshire, Barton Wright 0-6-0 shunts vans into the warehouse.

Fiddich made what would turn out to be its last appearance under my ownership.

I then had to ask, what should I do now? I have a virtually brand new exhibition layout that I cannot transport to exhibitions, which could not be reduced in size easily. I decided very reluctantly that I would have to sell it and fortunately I was able to find a buyer very quickly. I have become increasingly interested in 5″ gauge railways over the past few years, and I was on the point of abandoning O gauge modelling altogether.

During the following winter months I looked at all the locomotives and rolling stock that I had built over the past 30 years and could not bear to think of selling them, so I turned my thoughts to a possible new exhibition layout. I was missing the buzz that you get exhibiting models that you have constructed, and chatting to the various types of people that you meet at exhibitions. I still had two baseboards - 56″ x 28″ - that had formed the hidden sidings at either end of my Watersmeet layout, another exhibition layout I had to dispose of, because it was too big for me to handle on my own.

The next question was, what type of layout to put on these baseboards? I have a number of Lancashire & Yorkshire and London Midland Region locomotives. I did not want to spend time building more locomotives, as I had enough already, so I decided the layout would be based on this region. I then recalled my visit to Goole Docks, nine months earlier; perfect! I had a huge number of photographs of the dock infrastructure, taken on that visit, I always try to build layouts based on photographs of actual locations. All my layouts are built to represent the late '50s or early '60s, and this would allow me to include the overhead coal railway.

The baseboards are constructed from 12mm plywood so they are strong, but light enough to carry into exhibition halls, even if you have to walk upstairs. Track is Peco, with hand-built points, the rail being soldered to copper clad sleepers. This system might not look as pretty as using plastic chairs for the sleepers, but the track is covered in dirt in goods yards and docks so the lack of them is not noticeable, and this is the cheapest method of constructing pointwork. I make as much use as possible of three-way points or double slips when building small layouts as they are great space savers. Two three-way points have been used here. In the past I have never enjoyed making pointwork, but in constructing them for this layout, I seemed to be making express progress, they were only taking about two or three hours to build. This was in complete contrast to working in 5″ gauge earlier in the year, where a point takes me 20 hours to complete.

Looking through the docks entrance gate, from the street, the Class 02 diesel stands in the siding.

Buildings are made from card, collected from a variety of sources, with indented brick plastic card glued on to it. There is a lot of free card available if you keep your eyes out for it, and it works well provided it is supported inside the buildings with triangles of card glued top and bottom in the corners. The dock has a plywood base, painted a grey/green colour with many layers of clear varnish brushed on to it. The boat was built from a study of photographs of those taken in the docks. It was constructed from two pieces of balsa wood at a total cost of £1.80. Although it is only three-quarter scale, it looks just right; if it had been built to its scale size it would have overpowered the whole model. The same principles were applied to the buildings, I measured up the water tank and enginemen's bothy on my visit to the docks, but having cut out cardboard to scale size, I realised that each building would have to be reduced to fit the available space. Dock warehouses are huge buildings and would need more room than I had available to model them to scale. The only bought-in items were the two small dock cranes, from Duncan Models, but I hope to replace them with ones that represent more accurately the cranes at Goole. The dozen or so seagulls are from Langley Models, the sacks on the dockside are from Ten Commandments and the rear arches from Buzz Models.

I have attempted a number of small cameos with figures around the layout. I am not sure if exhibition visitors notice these, although sometimes they receive comment, but they are an essential part of a model. I have tried to create some life-like features for people to look at even when no locomotives are moving

The 'Pug' stands outside the enginemens bothy. Steam locomotives working in the docks at Goole always used the engine lamp code of one lamp over each buffer.

A view across the dock, with the river barge loading its timber cargo,, whilst the 02 shunts in the background.

DUTCH RIVER DOCK TRACK PLAN

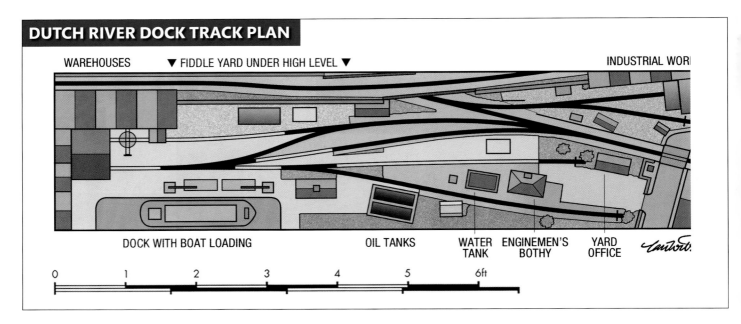

WAREHOUSES   ▼ FIDDLE YARD UNDER HIGH LEVEL ▼   INDUSTRIAL WORl

DOCK WITH BOAT LOADING   OIL TANKS   WATER   ENGINEMEN'S   YARD
TANK   BOTHY   OFFICE

0   1   2   3   4   5   6ft

around the layout, although many visitors just seem to concentrate on the movements and ignore the small details. The figures are from various sources, usually purchased at one of the Gauge O Guild Trade Shows.

The stock seen on the model has performed, over the past 20 years or so, on various exhibition layouts that I have constructed. The main locomotives that are seen in use are the 'Jinty', and the 'Pug', supported by an 02 and 08 diesel, all locomotive types that shunted at Goole Docks at one time or another. All locomotives are scratch-built from brass with the exception of the 08. Goole shed played host

to a wide variety of locomotives, I have seen photographs of J50s, J10s, J72s and even a T1 4-8-0 North Eastern tank locomotive there, in addition to the London Midland region types and many 'Austerity' 2-8-0s. I have under construction a J50, being constructed in plastic card, which was started for a previous layout some ten years ago, so I now have an incentive to complete it. When it is finished, I might build a T1, as this would be a challenge as I have not made such a large tank locomotive before, and you do not see many examples on the model railway scene. They did not actually shunt in the docks, they were used not far away, at the

Gascoigne Wood marshalling yards at Selby. The class finished their days at Tyne Dock.

I was brought up living 50 yards from the Lancashire & Yorkshire main line, over which a succession of long coal trains passed every few hours, bringing coal from Yorkshire to Lancashire. Since this time, I have always had more of an interest in freight locomotives rather than express passenger locomotives and have built a large number of, mainly ex-LMS large freight locomotives. Although the layout is small, I sometimes introduce a large freight locomotive to do some shunting at exhibitions, which gives the operator new problems to solve

The crew of the Class 08 shunter take a break whilst their locomotive ticks over in the background.

A view from the roof of a warehouse, along the yard.

on the tight head shunts, but more often an ex-L&Y 0-6-0 locomotive is used as the main line engine, working to and from the hidden siding.

The rolling stock consists of mainly open wagons and vans, many of them dating from my earliest days in O gauge in the 1970s. They are a mixture of kits and scratch-built, these being in plastic card or balsa wood. The layout has two sidings to the right and two to the left, so shunting can take place in either direction. In addition there is a small industrial works in the right corner, which is shunted by a Hibberd industrial diesel locomotive. As a youngster, having spent many hours during the holidays and at weekends in the signal box in which my Uncle Tommy worked during the 1950s, I learnt the vital importance of signalling on the railways. Signals are one of the first things I look for on a model railway and I always include working examples in any model I build. There is not a lot of scope for signals on this layout but there are two ground dollies and one home signal.

As on many layouts nowadays, some use is made of electronics, which provide a focal point if no stock is moving. There is a fire in the enginemen's bothy and a welder in the industrial building. I hope to make the level crossing gates work at a later date. I think that it is important to have plans to constantly improve the layout because this enables you to maintain interest in it.

The name comes from the man-made waterway, built by Dutch engineers, which connected the River Humber with the inland waterway system, thus allowing goods to be transported by water to the industrial towns and cities of Yorkshire. On a visit to the docks today, you will see numerous large stocks of imported timber, and I saw a huge pile of broken glass on the dock side having been unloaded from a Trinidad registered ship, which I assume was to be taken for melting down and recycling. Such a pile represented on the model may make an interesting feature, if I can find a way of modelling broken glass. There is also traffic in steel coil. I hope that circumstances will allow me to exhibit this layout for a longer time than the previous one and that I can improve it over the years. My hope at each exhibition that I take it to is that someone will look at it, feel that they can do better, and make the effort to prove they can, thus moving our hobby forward. **BRM**

A van is halted at the street level crossing as the 'Pug' passes by.

Building a Furness 'Seagull'

John Cockcroft describes construction of a Sharp Stewart 4-4-0 from the Dragon Models 7mm scale kit. *Model photography by the author.*

I don't know about you, but I think the Lake District is one of the most attractive landscapes in Britain and the thought of one of these neat little engines, blurred with happy thoughts of the Lakes, produced one of my overwhelming whims to get the kit and build the model! Another reason for my impulse is that the only other model of one of these locos that I have seen, was a scratch-built version on the late David Jenkinson's Kendal Branch layout – that in its way was as inspirational as the Lake District!

The kit is etched-brass and nickel silver with lost wax brass castings, including the otherwise challenging firebox front, and a number of clean white metal castings for boiler fittings, etc. Turned brass bearings and hand rail knobs complete the kit. The instructions comprise background notes and a brief history of the locos in Cambrian and Furness versions, though most of the information is on the Cambrian. I had to make a considerable number of alterations, particularly on the tender, to conform with the photographs of the Furness prototype. I can't say whether Cambrian modellers will encounter the same problem. The instructions wisely advise you to get a good photo of the loco you intend to model because of the number of detail differences. One thing to watch is that on many of the engines substantial bogie wheel splashers were fitted to the frames that on a model will severely restrict side movement of the bogie. These were removed from the Furness engines by LMS days.

The instructions comprise a running text that refers to a comprehensive series of colour photographs of the relevant part of the construction process. A drawing of the loco and tender is supplied but is to 10mm scale. I made photocopies to 7mm scale and found them of much more use.

I bought Slater's wheels as advised in the kit but please note that the recommended drivers have a smaller crank throw than normal so that the coupling rods will clear the loco body – so be careful if you propose using cast iron wheels. I used an ABC 'Minibox' motor/gear box that I hoped would fit into the firebox and drive the front driving axle, the rear axle being a bit too close to the cab floor for comfort.

The tender

I started with the tender which looked simple enough! With any 4-4-0 the problem is that the driving wheels are at the back and the whole front end sits on the bogie. Furthermore the boiler is the heaviest part and offers most opportunity to add weight, but is mostly in front of the drivers - the bit that is available is full of motor! This makes these locos front heavy and needs addressing if performance is not to be affected.

First, fit as much lead as possible in the rear part of the body as far forward as the front driving axle. Second, make sure that the front bogie is well sprung so that it throws some of the weight backwards onto the drivers, but not so as it lifts them off the track! Third, I like to compensate the

drivers by making one axle rigid and the other pivot over a rod or beam at the centre of the axle. This improves adhesion but more importantly electrical pick up. Finally I try to make the tender so that the rear axle is the only load bearing point and the other two axles are lightly sprung, but the front of the tender is arranged to sit on the back of the loco. Then put lead in the front part of the tender, which transfers its weight onto the rear of the loco and holds it down, increasing adhesion on the drivers.

Commencing with the tender sub-frame, I cut away the top part of the holes for the bearings on the front two axles and soldered an approximately 5cm length of 0.7mm brass wire to the inside of the frames back from the bearing, the other end being soldered to the top of the bearing, pushing it downwards and acting as a light spring. I did this while the etches were still flat - then folded up the sides and ends and soldered them to form the box-like sub-frame. To ensure that the bearings were in line with the axles I put an axle through them when I soldered them in place. The frames are quite narrow and

No.10133 in not so clean condition at Barrow in Furness in 1924. Notice that there is no lubricator on the dome. RJ Essery

I soldered the rear bearings well out from the frames to reduce side play. The other bearings, being held only by the wire springs were fitted close to the frames and the side play of the wheels controlled by various washers.

Next I soldered up the brake hanger and shoe units. These are handed but not really etched as such. Then I discovered an error - the drawing showed that the shoes should be in line with the axles with the long part at the top. The photos clearly showed the brakes fitted the wrong way up! I repositioned the hanger wires 3mm higher up the frames so that the shoes were in the right position. The rest of the brake gear went in without a problem.

I did a lot of work on the body components before making a single soldered joint. After my brake hanger experience I slipped into suspicious mode and checked everything I could in advance so as to try not to end up being tricked into a hard to solve mess by another inaccuracy. The tender sides were about 3mm shorter than in the drawing but my main worry was that the lost wax casting for the front handrails and brake stanchion would not fit because of this – that worry was unfounded!

Another issue was the position of the tender body relative to the footplate which has to be determined by the modeller. I marked the sides at equal distances from the sides of the footplate and put a short line at the front end where the tender side etch ended.

I formed the curved flares on the top of the tank sides next. There is no attempt in the kit to etch a curve to the corners of the flare on either the end or sides and you have to carefully file the corners to fit to the side flare and make a nice neat join below. I only filed the tender back etch at this stage because the sides can be done later when they are assembled – remember that a mess on the back is easier to hide than one on the sides.

At this point I considered how at the painting stage I would be able to line the lower part of the tender tank where it is behind the outside springs. I resolved that the tank would have to be removable. This presented me with the issue of the nice lost wax handrails at the front – whether they should be part of the body or be attached to the footplate. I concluded that they would be stronger if they were soldered to the tank at the top and fitted into holes in the footplate at the bottom, so a careful measuring exercise followed and I drilled three holes on the left side and two on the right. I had still not touched the body with the soldering iron!

To make the tender body removable I

No.10134 in clean condition showing off the LMS livery and lining very well - notice the lubricator on the dome. The lining is more elaborate thatn the standard LMS/MR style. *John Cockcroft collection*

Unlike in the USA, where most locomotives operated by even the bigger railway companies were bought off the peg from specialist locomotive builders, British railways usually either built their own or had outside builders construct locomotives to designs supplied to them. From a modellers point of view it is very unusual to be able to produce a kit that suits more than one railway company. So this model is a very rare bird indeed!

These lovely, neat little locomotives were produced by Sharp Stewart for the Cambrian Railways in 1878 when two were ordered, with another two in 1886. However, when another four were built in 1890/1 they were completed late and the Cambrian refused to take them, so they were sold instead to the Furness

Railway who numbered them 120-123. For some reason they were nicknamed 'Seagulls'. Oddly enough the Cambrian bought two more in 1891 making a class of six in total. So modellers have a choice of either Wales or Cumbria, and the models can be painted in black, russet red, crimson lake, or green.

A problem for later Cambrian or GWR modellers is that between 1910 and 1916 their locos were reboilered and lost their attractive raised fireboxes. Dragon Models also produce a kit with the later boiler, but it would not be beyond the more experienced modeller to make a replacement for this kit. Furness or LMS locos remained as original through to scrapping, all being scrapped between 1922 and 1930.

drilled four 1.5mm holes in the base and four matching holes in the footplate. I then tapped the holes in the tank base 2M and opened out those in the footplate to 2mm and countersunk them. I could then use 2M countersunk screws to remove the tender tank for painting.

The other thing I did was drill the sub-frame fixing holes in the footplate to 1.5 mm and tap them 2M and use 2M nylon bolts for the fixing. By sticking a layer of insulation tape on the top of the sub-frame and using the nylon bolts I effectively isolated the sub-frame from the body and made installation of electrical pick-up much easier.

I commenced construction of the tender body with the footplate and frames, which is my preferred method. There are two sets of frames in the kit so choose the right one using photographic evidence. I noted a variation in the outside frames on the Furness locos, this being that the brake cross shaft appears to be mounted above the lower front step, not on the end of the projecting part of the frame front as in the kit, I altered the front step area to match the photos.

Construction proper began by soldering the outside frames into the grooves in the footplate. I then discovered that the front draw beam etch fits between the frames but the draw beam on the prototype projects out to the full width of the footplate. So I soldered the draw beam in place and then made up another from scrap etch. I was not bothered about the slot for the coupling link because my arrangement will have to transfer the weight of the tender to the loco.

Next I observed from the photos that the rear buffer beam on the Furness locos was a thick wooden affair that projects beyond the footplate, but the one in the kit represents a thin steel type. The instructions state there were many variations so a good photo of your chosen prototype is vital. To represent this I used 2mm square brass tube soldered to the top and sides of the buffer beam. By using full temperature solder for attaching the tube, and 145° solder to attach the unit to the frames I minimised the danger of accidental melting of joints. I sat back to admire my work when the kit suddenly leaped out and bit me! The bottom of the buffer beam projected

about 2mm below the rear part of the frames, whereas the drawing and photos showed that frames and buffer beam were the same depth, so the frames had to be made deeper. This is very annoying as a new section of frame has to be inserted, and both the incorrect original and the correct prototype are subtly curved up to the axleguard so I had to file and shape this by eye. Then I soldered some small rectangles of waste behind the frames against which I could solder the new extensions. I used full melt solder for all the frame extension and buffer beam construction, but 145° solder for attaching the buffer beam without unsoldering all my work.

My next observation was that there are guard irons on the back of the tender on the photos but none in the kit or on the drawing. I used a clear side view of a Furness four wheeled tender, identical in detail to the six wheel version in the kit, and discovered that the guard irons fit from inside the frames and flare out to line up with the wheels. I soldered them to the back corners of the tender sub-frame with the curve commencing in line with the bottom of the frame. Then I noted that there is a sloping lidded tool box at the rear of the tender footplate that stretches the full width of the body as far back as the buffer beam. This is definitely a Furness variation and features on all the four wheel tenders as well as this six wheel version, but is absent from the kit.

I used photos to draw in the side and therefore the rear and top. Though I cut out the parts from more scrap etch, I didn't assemble them at this stage. They look to be riveted on the top and back edges - so I riveted them!

The springs are quite clean white metal castings but I was initially anxious that the thin shackles and main locating rod would be too weak and easily damaged during handling. In the end, however, the photos showed that the bottom of the springs were almost in contact with the footplate and once soldered in place they were very strong. The holes in the footplate for the hangers are a fraction too close together so I bent the shackle castings on the ends of the springs inwards then bent the hanger rods vertical again so that they fit in the holes. I soldered them in place from under the footplate using 145° solder but was careful not to touch the white metal parts with the iron. With plenty of flux the solder shot onto the castings and I avoided melting any of them. Finally, I constructed what I thought the front brake cross shaft and operating rod looked like from photos. The sub-frame is so short that there is lots of room at either end to mess about with cross shafts and still get the thing in and out easily.

The tender body is built differently to any other I have made and consists of a built-up inner unit assembled on a base plate, with internal bulkheads and inner sides that support the tender top. The top curves down to the coal space at the front. As mentioned earlier, one advantage of this method is that the body can be made as a separate unit that can be detached for painting. I had pre-drilled and tapped the base with this in mind so assembled the whole top on a flat

surface, but kept checking it against the footplate as I went along. The bulkheads soldered to the base accurately and the inner sides fitted equally well making a super strong brick-like structure. From my experience with the kit I was anxious that the tender sides and ends should be as well fitting and neat as possible and so next measured the back against the inner structure. I was not surprised to find it was about 1.5mm wider than the inner, and all other components that go across the tender body. I soldered it as centrally as possible to the rear of the inner structure and filed the edges until they were flush with the inner sides. I next fitted the sides making sure the whole unit was on a dead flat surface, particularly ensuring that the rear corner was tight and did not project at the rear. I laminated both sides to the inner structure. I am not all that happy that the thin outer etch seals in a load of flux and other corrosives behind it, but you have no choice!

Another peculiar feature of the design is that the very thin sides are supported on a brick-like inner for much of their length but are like tissue at the front and can be easily damaged by handling even when the front bulkhead is in place. I resolved to put some strengthening in place later.

The tender top was first curved then riveted in order to avoid damaging rivets when bending it. Again the use of a riveting tool is most desirable for both ease and evenness of rivet sizes. I found the kit has a tendency to build in problems even if you think you have done everything perfectly. This reared its head when I had soldered in the tender top and found a gap of around 1mm at one side towards the rear of the tender even though I had to file it a little towards the front where it curved down in order to get it to fit between the sides. I cut and filed a thin strip of brass to fill this gap. Because the sides and the tender front are half-etched they are quite floppy and vulnerable, mainly because I was not soldering them to the footplate. I cut a rectangle of scrap etch and soldered it into the bottom of the coal space, that solved that problem and

also made a good base for the lead weighting I fitted in later.

Next I assembled the rear tool box, earlier cut from scrap etch, across the tender rear. I only fitted one of the sandboxes into the front corner of the coal space as I intended to fill the space with lead and didn't want to lose weight. The tank was then test fitted to the footplate unit and after a slight kiss with the file it sat with barely a hairline gap.

On looking at the prototype photos I noticed three additional variations from the kit that needed attention. First there is on the Furness tenders a curved topped tool box that sits inside the front of the coal space on the right-hand side. I fitted a cast version, though I had to cut it down a little as it was too long. Secondly, the tender brake was operated by a hand wheel, not a handle as represented by the lost wax casting in the kit. This I bought from Laurie Griffin, and after clipping off the original brake handle and drilling the wheel, soldered it on the top of the casting with a short length of wire soldered to the rim as a handle.

The third variation was more annoying. The axleboxes supplied are not the type that appear in the photos. The Furness type is a tall rectangular box with stepped-in sides so I had to make these. I made a long strip of two layers of brass, the top one narrower than the bottom soldered with Carr's high temperature solder, then cut them to length using a piercing saw, soldered in place using 145° solder so that they didn't come apart.

First thoughts on the locomotive

After all the changes I had to make on the tender I anticipated an even more imaginative time with the more complex loco. I have certain ways of building locos that usually involve some modification to kits, so I could only blame myself for much of what I was expecting! Whenever I could I checked the fit, length or diameter of any component against the drawing, but more

The model certainly captures the elegant Victorian lines of the prototype very well.

Furness Railway Headlight Codes - 1899

Taken from the Supplement to the Working Time Table

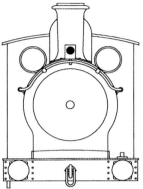

1. Light Engine or Shunting Engine in station yard (red tail lamp).

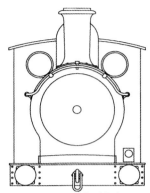

2. Passenger, Mixed Train or Special Fish.

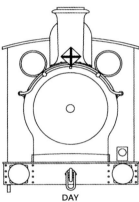

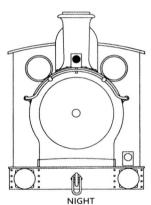

DAY — NIGHT

2. Passenger, Mixed Train or Special Fish - when running Empty, Relief or Special Train.

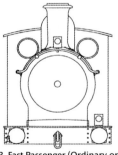

3. Fast Passenger (Ordinary or Special or Breakdown).

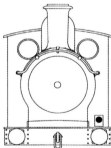

4. Goods or Ballast Train.

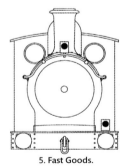

5. Fast Goods.

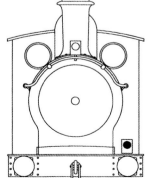

DAY — NIGHT

6. Express Goods, Special Cattle or Breakdown Train.

importantly against the other parts of the kit!

The first two parts I extracted from the fret were the footplate and the frames, as a mismatch here would be a source of pain and rage when the two were put together. I kept them close and built both in parallel whenever I could. The chassis and body are nickel silver which is a good thing because though nickel silver is a bit harder to bend and form, it is less prone to distortion and does not conduct heat as quickly as brass making it a bit easier to solder. The frames come as a 'U'-shape fold up with cross spacers at the rear and above the bogie pivot area. There appear to be no bulkheads supplied to strengthen this structure though it may be supported by later construction including cross wires for brake gear, etc. However, I wanted to pivot the rear driving axle to give some compensation, and needed to fit a rod longitudinally along the centre line on which the axle could rest but be free to pivot. So I inserted a couple of bulkheads across the chassis, one either side of the rear driving axle, each with a hole drilled a clearance fit for a length of 1.3mm diameter steel wire positioned to bear on the top of the driving axle. I soldered the wire into the bulkheads whilst ensuring it was resting on the axle which was temporarily located in position. In this way the pivoted axle would sit at the right height and the chassis should be level. I was then able to deal with the bearings so that they could move up and down in a vertical direction only.

I used Fourtrack Models reasonably priced and highly effective hornguide and bearings to provide the movement of the axle. I cut them down on one side to clear the nearby bulkhead, and used a piercing saw to cut a slot in the frames so the bearing could move freely. Next I laminated the coupling rods – I used three layers on each even though the instructions refer to only two layers. A good flood of solder ensured that the top edge and ends could be filed smooth with no hint of laminates.

I have some special axles that have the ends turned down to fit through crank pin holes and use them to position the bearings accurately by fitting them through the bearings and putting the ends through the crank pin holes in the rods. When the rods are fitted snugly and the bearings are held in the frames they can be soldered in place and are sure to be at the same spacing as the holes in the rods. In this case the rear bearings were in hornguides and can move up and down and it was the hornguides that I soldered to the frames. Because the bearings kept falling out I soldered a wire keeper under each of them. Next I tested the chassis with the wheels, coupling rods and motor in place using crocodile clips to the motor terminals and after a little opening out of the crank pin holes the chassis ran smoothly.

I fitted the ash pan etching but curved the bottom skirt under in the way that is visible on photos of the prototype. Then I assembled the bogie which is quite complicated with white metal representations of bearing blocks and etched equalizing beams and springs.

I simply followed the instructions and it went together very well - just make sure it is true by checking on a sheet of glass that it will not rock. I also inserted another home made bulkhead vertically at the rear of the front cross spacer.

This would form the basis of any representation of the inside motion that I chose to fit at a later time. Next I went on to build the basic body in order to check that the motor would fit and enable me to arrange the bogie pivot and body fixing screws.

Body

The footplate, as is almost inevitable on a loco with big wheels and small coupling rod splashers almost to the edge, is very flimsy when cut out of the fret. So, before anything else, I firmed it all up by fitting the valances, buffer beam and drag beam. There are two types of valance depending on the shape of the rear step plate and both are on the fret. They come with the curious fold down plates that are meant to be soldered under the footplate. They are virtually useless and make forming a sharp and neat joint where the valance meets the footplate much more difficult so I removed them. I fitted the front buffer beam first because the overhang is critical, then found that the valance etch is about 2.5mm short if the rear is placed at the correct location at the rear of the footplate. I discovered it is the footplate that is too long so had to shorten the footplate.

As recommended in the instructions I used lengths of thin waste etch for the cab cut-out beading. Roughly pre-formed it was tack soldered, then carefully seamed tight to the cab side shape and filed and fibre glass brushed into a neat representation of the real thing. Don't forget to leave about 3mm at the bottom end to take the top of the cab stanchion.

The beading round the splashers and on the cab sides is etched in brass so that modellers of some periods can have it polished. I tinned the back of the beadings with full temperature solder and then used the tacky paste of Powerflow flux to hold the beading in place while I tack soldered one end and then soldered the rest in place. I followed the instructions and assembled the cab front to the sides, ensuring they were both square and level. There are some huge tags on the front and sides so I cut them

Locomotive body and chassis completed.

off to less than 1mm deep, and removed those on the cab front entirely as they missed the slots when the sides were in position on the footplate. The sides were a little narrow compared to the slots in the footplate but by positioning them equally and using a fillet of solder to fill the gaps I got the cab in place.

The instructions recommend that the boiler and firebox unit are located next, but I opted to solder the splasher sides into place on the footplate, followed by the tops so that each part can be fitted accurately and tightly at each stage ensuring a good finish where it matters. I then fitted the small coupling rod splashers at the sides of the cab side and front splashers. Again I fitted the fronts first, then the curved tops, forming them over a brass bar and carefully filing and fettling to fit the footplate and both sides of the splasher.

Next I moved onto the firebox. Long after fitting it to the loco I discovered that the firebox etching is about 3mm too long but it was too late to correct this so I have to live with it. Shortening it would involve a number of alterations to the rest of the loco body, but apart from shortening the footplate I decided to live with the error. The firebox front is a really nice lost wax brass casting that requires only a little cleaning up to represent the curved brass front of the prototype very effectively. As I was driving the loco from the front axle I had to saw out the bottom of the casting to clear the gearbox. I cut almost all the way through but left it complete to be stronger if I had to use a bit of force to hold the wrapper in place as I soldered it. It has a flange behind to take the etched wrapper which has to be formed to match its profile. I would have welcomed a plain etched back end for the firebox that could be lined up with the hole already etched in the cab front but I found that with patience the wrapper can be made to fit the rebate at the front exactly and a good fillet of solder secured a solid and very neat join. Check that the bottom edges are both parallel and at right angles to the front and you can then commence fitting the unit onto the loco body.

Fitting is a simple exercise in patience and filing – in that order. Avoid over enthusiasm with the file that leaves gaps to fill after. I scribed a line on the front of the cab where the firebox should come to and discovered that once I had got the unit to fit on the footplate it was a millimetre or so high so scribed and filed to a line at the bottom of each side to get it to sit exactly right. I then scribed the shape of the splasher tops on the sides of the firebox and cut it to shape to clear the wheels, then soldered the firebox unit to the footplate, splashers and cab front.

I checked the pre-rolled boiler was the right diameter according to the drawing when the gap at the bottom was pushed closed. It was perfect and fitted the flange on the front casting of the firebox like a glove, so I soldered along the seam but strengthened the join with a strip

The tender body and sub-chassis.

THE AMERICAN SYSTEM OF PICK-UP

This is a way of getting engines to pick up without pick-ups - you pick up through the wheels on the loco and return through the wheels of the tender. I shorted out the plastic centres of the Slater's wheels on one side of each axle by drilling a fine hole in the rim and the brass hub, then made a groove down the adjacent spoke. I then quickly soldered a short length of copper wire into the holes at each end being careful not to distort or melt the plastic centre. Using this system it is usual for the insulated wheels on the loco to be on the right and those on the tender on the left (looking forward from the cab). I soldered one of the leads from the motor onto the frames and the other to a square of circuit board glued under the chassis. Make sure that the loco is wired so that it goes forward when all the other locos you own go forward. We don't need surprises when starting a train!

I soldered a length of brass tube under the tender chassis and cut a length of copper wire to fit snugly in the tube as a removable plug. Finally I soldered a length of wire from the circuit board to the copper wire plug. The chassis ran, provided the loco and tender chassis did not touch. As noted earlier I ensured that the loco and tender chassis were attached by 2M nylon screws to eliminate any short circuit in the fixing. I then stuck a carefully cut length of electrical insulation tape over the top of both chassis where they would otherwise touch the bodies.

As the two bodies are electrically isolated from the chassis I could arrange the tender link in my normal way by simply soldering a thick rod on the front drawbeam of the tender to act as a draw pin, and fit a flat plate projecting from under the drawbeam on the loco. This plate is arranged so that the underside of the drawbeam of the tender sits on it at exactly the correct height. A short slot in the plate takes the draw pin and allows some movement, but the plate takes the weight of the front of the tender, holding the back of the loco down and increasing adhesion. Because it is a plate, it discourages any tendency for the tender to twist down on either side.

You can use a hinged fall plate on the back of the loco to hide the gap but it gets in the way when hooking the tender onto the plate - I usually solder the fall plate to the tender and make it look as though it is attached to the loco! When all this was finished and the lead and plug between the loco and tender were connected, the model ran very well from first testing.

of waste etch soldered inside along the seam line. Next, I soldered on the pre-rolled overlay that builds up the smokebox thickness under the outer wrapper. To make sure it was both tight to the boiler and not spiralled I held it in place with a couple of lengths of copper wire wrapped round and twisted tight at the ends. A combination of soldering iron and blow torch made sure the seams were flooded with solder and really tight.

What I missed was that the wrapper etch is too wide. While the etches are flat, lay the outer wrapper over the inner, line up the fronts and mark a line on the inner about 1mm back from the outer wrapper edge and cut off the surplus. I had to saw to a mark with everything soldered to the boiler and then unsolder the surplus with carefully applied blow torch and soldering iron – a fraught and unpleasant exercise! I scribed a mark on top of the smokebox and at the top of the smokebox front etch and soldered it in place by first tack soldering and then seaming when I was sure it was even all round.

The smokebox wrapper is half-etched with the rivets along both edges. The best way to deal with it is to form the tight curves that tuck into the bottom flares first, then form the main bend. I tack soldered the wrapper to the top of the smokebox then held it in close down one side and into the shape of the smokebox front and tacked there. You may have to move the bend of the flare upwards a little as you go on but that is no problem. Then do the other side and finally seam all the way round front and rear, but leave part of the rear unsoldered because you have to cut the back of the smokebox saddle from an etch on the sheet as per the instructions and you want to be able to fit that without having to unsolder parts of the wrapper. The wrapper is a bit overlong which is a good thing. You can file off the surplus after it is fitted.

I made a number of alterations to how the bogie was mounted and sprung, I would hardly call these sophisticated but they were aimed at making sure that the front of the engine was supported and guided by the bogie. The main way I do this is to ensure that the bogie has some weight on it but that the weight is counteracted by a good spring. The effect of the weight and the spring is to make the bogie hold the track and give some steer to the front of the loco without resorting to side control springs.

The bogie pivot is an 8BA bolt soldered to the horizontal chassis spacer under the smokebox. I marked the location and then messed with it until it was vertical and central. Over this I slid a length of tube that would project a bit below the bogie pivot plate but left a bit of the bolt showing so a nut could be tightly screwed onto it. The spring fits over the tube and a washer sits on it, acting as a rubbing plate on the bogie. I extended the pivot hole in the bogie sideways so that it was a slot about 6-7mm wide in which the tube was free to slide. The assembly was then retained by a washer and nut. I had to mess about with the spring so that its pressure was just right at the correct ride height. To control the back end of the bogie from excessive movement causing the wheels to short on the frames I soldered two short lengths of 0.7mm wire vertically from inside the bogie frames so that they fitted

The late David Jenkinson argued that had his Kendal branch actually been built, there might have been a case for keeping at least one of the Sharp Stewart 4-4-0s to work the line. No.10133 was built by Peter Everton and painted in pre-1928 livery by Larry Goddard. *Tony Wright*

between the loco frames preventing excessive side play but leaving a good deal of slop. In this way the rear of the bogie is controlled, the pivot can slide sideways in the slot and there is a lot of side movement enabled at the front where it is needed.

I then detailed the chassis - I found some castings for the nozzles of the steam sanders and added a couple of wires to represent sand and steam pipes. I noticed some pipes and what look like valves on the side of the firebox below the footplate and used 1mm brass wire soldered on the side to represent them. I used a spare white metal whistle casting from my scrap box to represent the valve on the right-hand side. Between the frames I messed about with scrap etch to fill the space under the boiler with slide bar and valve gear impressions. The rest of the detail is as in the kit. The chassis was sprayed with Halford's primer, then matt black and it was time to get the loco running!

Detailing and painting

I could now move onto the home run by detailing the loco body. Most of the parts in the kit are covered by the instructions and fitted pretty much as expected. I filed the cab roof gutter etches once they were in place to make

Have your say! Visit our new Forum at: **www.RMweb.co.uk**

them look like those on the photo. The front steps appear to have a slightly different shape on the Furness locos to those supplied in the kit so I filed the top into a tighter radius curve where they meet the valance. The steps are not marked or half etched on the back plate and you have to be careful with fitting these to get them correctly spaced and horizontal in both directions – a bit of a fiddly job! Lamp irons are spare etch strip as those supplied appear to be Cambrian. I noticed that the train heating and vacuum brake pipes were carried along the loco under the valance and replicated this using 1.2 mm brass wire tacked to the valance and behind the steps.

Turned washout plugs are provided in the kit but looking at photos of the locos in LMS days they appear to be projecting bolts. I soldered in lengths of 1.2 mm wire and clipped them off about 1.5 mm proud of the firebox then filed them to a flat top. A few strokes of the file on the sides gave them a square effect. An ejector pipe runs along the right side of the boiler and I made this from tube with a washer on the smokebox side and a loop of wire round the tube soldered liberally to represent the cast elbow on the prototype. I replaced the steam heat and vac pipes with lost wax versions from my scrap collection.

I reduced the rim of the chimney a little and tried to clean out the inside of the top to get rid of a casting ridge inside. I used two-part epoxy glue to attach the chimney and dome, etc. The whistle on these engines is of the overhead lever type so I adapted a Laurie Griffin casting using wire and brass strip. I made the cab backhead and floor as one unit by soldering a brass floor plate to the bottom of the backhead. The unit is secured by a bolt through the backhead into the cab front. The reversing lever was soldered, and cab floor timbers glued, to the brass floor plate. The remainder are covered by the instructions perfectly well without my comment, and with one mighty bound the engine was finished!

I painted the model in early LMS livery, which suits it very well. I found a number of photos of 10133 and 10134 and noticed that the Furness painter's interpretation of the lining was different to the Midland standard from which it was derived. The lining follows the cab front rather than being carried round the eves of the cab front, the lines follow the cab front down over the splasher top then round the inside edge of the splasher and over the top of the firebox. Unlike the Furness livery there is no polished brass on the splasher rims and the curved front edge of the firebox, but the small

coupling rod splashers have neat little lines on them, as do the ends of the buffer plank.

I used Halfords Satin Black and their Rover Damask Red from a spray can to get the basic colour onto the model. It was then lined black and yellow using a ruling pen. For LMS yellow lining I use Humbrol gloss yellow enriched with their gloss red and let down to a rich ochre by adding black until it ceases to jump out at me! Numbers are from the HMRS LMS gold sheet and Guilplates supplied a smoke box number plate. I varnished the model with a mix of Ronseal gloss and satin polyurethane varnish sprayed using my Iwata airbrush. I lightly weathered the model to a used but clean look using stiff brushes and a stiff drink to give me courage to mess up all my work!

After cleaning up the wheels and oiling all working parts I reassembled the model. It seems to run really well, though I have yet to test it on tight curves to see how tolerant it is! I am annoyed by the overlong firebox even though it looks better than the original, but the model captures the elegant Victorian lines of the prototype very well and it is a pleasure to see it swinging along my test track with effortless grace. It's the next best thing to going to Grange-over-Sands in 1924 and seeing the real thing come round the curve by Morecambe Bay. **BRM**

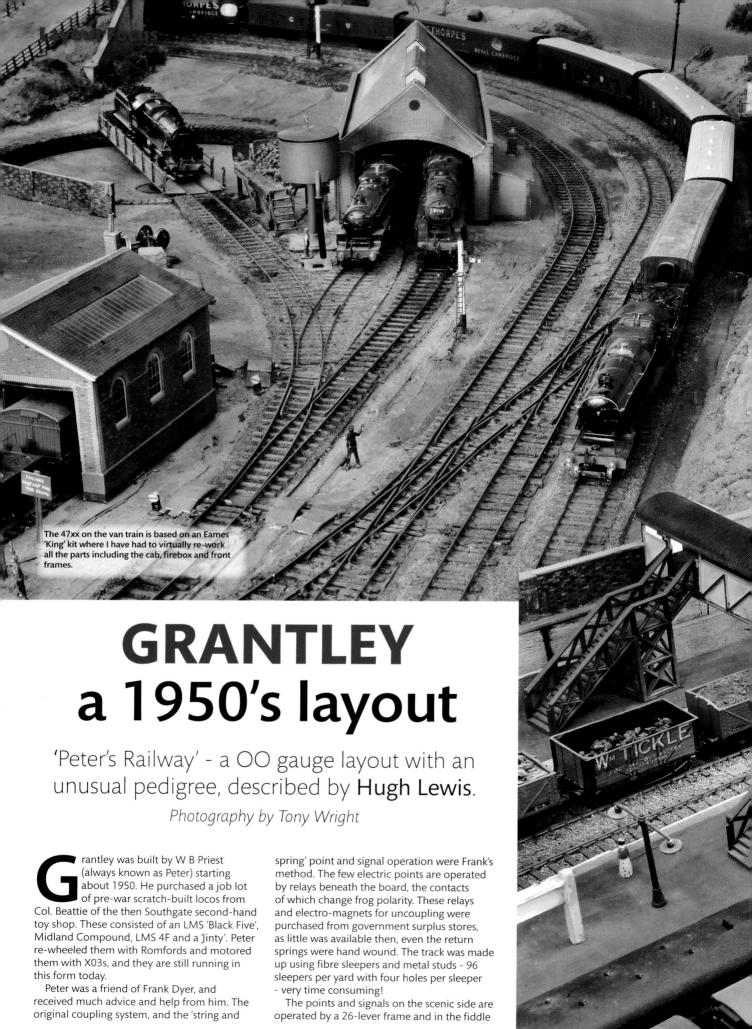

The 47xx on the van train is based on an Eames 'King' kit where I have had to virtually re-work all the parts including the cab, firebox and front frames.

GRANTLEY
a 1950's layout

'Peter's Railway' - a OO gauge layout with an unusual pedigree, described by **Hugh Lewis**.

Photography by Tony Wright

Grantley was built by W B Priest (always known as Peter) starting about 1950. He purchased a job lot of pre-war scratch-built locos from Col. Beattie of the then Southgate second-hand toy shop. These consisted of an LMS 'Black Five', Midland Compound, LMS 4F and a 'Jinty'. Peter re-wheeled them with Romfords and motored them with X03s, and they are still running in this form today.

Peter was a friend of Frank Dyer, and received much advice and help from him. The original coupling system, and the 'string and spring' point and signal operation were Frank's method. The few electric points are operated by relays beneath the board, the contacts of which change frog polarity. These relays and electro-magnets for uncoupling were purchased from government surplus stores, as little was available then, even the return springs were hand wound. The track was made up using fibre sleepers and metal studs - 96 sleepers per yard with four holes per sleeper - very time consuming!

The points and signals on the scenic side are operated by a 26-lever frame and in the fiddle

Have your say! Visit our new Forum at: **www.RMweb.co.uk**

yard by 12 and 17-lever frames. The electrics are by section and sub-section with a common return. Any combination of sections may be selected to any of the four controllers. Two of the controllers are original 'home-made' with full or half-wave facility, with or without smoothing.

The scenery uses all sorts of packing to create the basic shape, this was then covered with strips of newspaper soaked in dilute glue and/or plaster, forming a hard surface when set, and then painted and covered with various scatter materials - dried tea leaves, sand, etc. Trees were made from twigs, and bushes from moss raked from the lawn. Buildings were scratch-built but later replaced by card and plastic kits as they became available. The turntable is hand-operated by a system of Meccano bits and pieces. It is a railway of the 1950s and anything that could be adapted or made up was used.

I met Peter in 1961 through his sons, who are both still friends of mine, and with our common interest in railways we became

The engine shed with two 'Black Fives', that on the right is Peter's pre-war scratch built loco, the other is a K's kit with my own frames and Romford wheels.

A K's Garratt with two motors - one to haul the train! The tank is K's body kit of an LNWR 2-4-2 again with my frames and Romford wheels.

friends. Over the years I made several LMS engines to run on the railway as well as my own GWR stud.

The railway was moved and modified three times by Peter, the major changes being a simplification and reduction in size, and the adoption of Spratt & Winkle couplings.

When Peter died, aged 82, he left the railway to me so the railway had to be moved again. It was stored in my garage and shed for over a year until the loft room was ready for it. When first erected it smelt very damp and took some time to dry out. Reinstating the trackwork was fairly straightforward but the electrics took some time. I had some original diagrams for the relays used for junctions but most of the time it was a matter

ABOVE: A pre-war scratch built Midland Compound obtained in 1935 by Peter which he later re-motorised with new frames and wheels.

RIGHT: A K's 'Jubilee' with Romford wheels passes a 'Duchess' of similar provenance.

From right to left: a 28xx, 'City', curved frame 'Bulldog', Dean single, Dean goods, Armstrong 4-4-0, modified Bristol Models' 'Manor', 'Hall', 'Jubilee' and barely visible an 'Aberdare'. You can also see my part of the panel which mimics Peter's design.

ABOVE: 'Jubilee' and LNWR 2-4-2 tank with pre-war 4F in the background.

of lying on my back tracing and reconnecting wires. The string for points and signals was mostly replaced and adjusted, not stretching as much as expected. My friend Laurie came to help me reposition the somewhat delicate scenery, and at last we could see trains run again as Peter had. It took a while for the track to stabilise, but the room has good insulation and heating, therefore it is now as stable as track of this type can ever be expected to be. Having got the railway working, attention must now be given to the scenery and buildings. When this has been done the appearance will be considerably improved. **BRM**

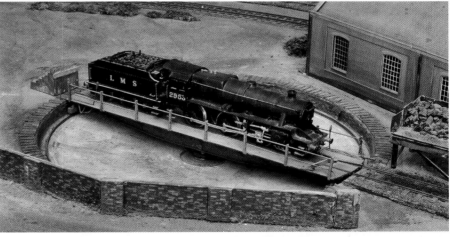

Above: K's Stanier Mogul on the turntable.

Left: Dock tank with K's body on my chassis. Most of the body kits were bought when the K's range was being re-engineered with new chassis and the bodies were being offered quite cheaply.

Above: Control panel showing the coloured sections and and on the left panel, the levers controlling the power to those sections.

Right: The bank of GEM levers controlling signals (red) and points (black).

The underside showing the string control, and wiring - 'the knitting'.

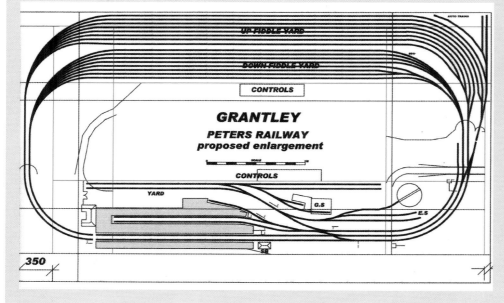

FIDDLE YARD

CONTROLS

GRANTLEY
PETERS RAILWAY

YARD

CONTROLS

G.S

E.S

SB

UP FIDDLE YARD

DOWN FIDDLE YARD

AUTO TRAINS

CONTROLS

GRANTLEY
PETERS RAILWAY
proposed enlargement

YARD

CONTROLS

G.S

E.S

SB

350

CHANGES

Since Tony Wright's photographic visit and after hearing comments as to how the railway could be modified without affecting Peter's original concept, I decided to bite the bullet and do it.

The idea was to make the fiddleyard easier to use by making the sidings through roads, thus avoiding the reverse shunting of long trains. The boards were divided and moved to give 600mm more depth and 250mm more width. This allowed four points to be inserted in the main circuits to give access and egress to previously dead end sidings.It also enabled some easing of the radii in tight spots.

On the scenic side only the tunnel mouths had to be slewed and a fairly plain insert of 250mm of embankment.

The oportunity was also taken to give the branch three hidden sidings. At an 'Ally Pally' show I picked up from the Model Railway Club sales stand three appropriate period relays for £5.00 suitable for point operation, and a three-way point also for £5.00. With these items, the last of Peter's spare points and some old Peco ones the work was completed. Some fine adjustments are still being made, but the result is very pleasing.

The aim for the future is to keep the railway sympathetically maintained, and hope that it will continue to give pleasure to many, though it is and always will be 'Peter's Railway'.

PYSTYLL GRAIG DDU

John and **Owen Gibbon** describe their minimum space O gauge
Taff Vale colliery line. *Photography by Tony Wright*

For those of you who are put off modelling in 7mm because of its size, don't worry, you can still build a layout that is interesting to operate and keeps the public attention at shows. The criteria for the layout was made based on the size we could get into the car, as well as the stock required to run it and our overnight bags, etc; This limited the overall length of the scenic section to 9' 0" and a width of 22", with the height set at 38" which we find convenient to operate at. An additonal 4' 0" x 1' 0" fiddle yard board gives a total overall length of 13' 0"

The railway company we decided upon was the Taff Vale as we have numerous items of rolling stock and locomotives to be able to satisfy our needs at a show. They would be borrowed from our somewhat larger layout Ynysybwl Fach, which has been published in *BRM* a few years ago, the photographs being taken by Tony Wright, who also took the ones for this article.

Anyway, that's the basic information out of the way, time to talk about the layout for those of you who are interested.

Baseboards

The baseboards are of plywood construction forming a rectangular tray with appropriate bracing. The legs are constructed from square section with bracing that folds up into the underside of the baseboard for transportation. The boards are connected by dowels from the EM Gauge Society for alignment, with case catches on the outside of the boards to lock them together. This makes for a quick assembly and knockdown at shows. The lighting gantry is made of timber with fluorescent lighting units in each half, which allows it to be folded for transportation, these just slot onto the main baseboards, with no clamping or bolting required.

The fiddle yard board where all the service to the layout is made is basically a flat clear area where cartridge loading of the trains is made. We have tried a different technique to most, in that the trays are made of square

A passenger train has just arrived at Pistyll Graig Ddu.

section rainwater downpipe, which is quartered, then paxolin section is glued onto two of the quarters and rail is then soldered in place. This forms a light tray for use, which becomes heavy when loaded with the 7mm scale models.

Layout design

The trackwork was drawn out on the baseboards to see what could be achieved in such a small space, it had to be interesting for both operator and viewer and as can be seen in the diagram of the trackwork there are a number of moves required for each train that arrives. This ranges from passenger traffic with various attached vehicles, goods trains which require the odd wagon or two to be removed and replaced, to the mineral traffic, in this case coal, where empties arrive and loaded wagons depart.

To accommodate all these manoeuvres, there is a platform face, goods loading dock, small goods yard and basic reception road for empty/ full coal wagons. In order that the coal wagons can be filled, there is a small screens area where the empty coal wagons are propelled and filled.

Buildings

The station building is representative of a Taff Vale type as is the small goods shed. The station building was constructed using Wills 4mm scale embossed stone sheet (see Paul Bason's article on how to use this), which gives a nice fine stone wall for the base of the building, the upper part being constructed of timber. The goods shed was built using corrugated sheets from Slater's 'Plastikard' range. Both buildings have a shell of foam board, which makes for a light building for transporting. The screens area has typical buildings for an early coal mine, the screens are modelled on the one at Bwlfa Dare in the Cynon Valley, the others taken from various sites in the valley.

Trackwork

As mentioned above, the trackwork was drawn out on the baseboards with the cork underlay being stuck to the board with double-sided tape.

Timber sleepers of scale thickness and length were cut from sheets of timber available at most model shops, for both the plain track and pointwork and positioned on the cork, again with double-sided tape. Some time was saved by the use of ready machined blades and noses ('frogs' as most of us call them), and the appropriate chairs for the bullhead rail purchased from C&L. The chairs, of the two-bolt variety, were slid onto the rail and then glued into place on the sleepers. However, there are other suppliers around that you can obtain these items from. Fishplates were of two types, brass and plastic. Brass ones were used to join the rails to give electrical conductivity and the plastic used where isolation sections were needed.

From the outset, we decided that all the pointwork was to be operated by motors/ solenoids, but they were all to be accessible at the rear of the boards behind or under the back scene. This would allow for either manual operation to keep the show running or replacement

Pistyll Graig Ddu station building is based on an early timber building at Treorchy .

without having to go on your hands and knees under the board to change them while under show conditions.

As we intended to run small locomotives, such as 0-6-0s and 0-6-2s, we were able to use smaller radius curves, the only problem being when it comes to shunting where you still need a small section of straight track to couple/ uncouple. Initially, we only intended to have one locomotive in power at any one time; however, with the screens area for filling empty coal wagons a need for another was made in this isolated area.

Railway Company

We mentioned earlier that our other layout was based in the main on the Taff Vale Railway and so all the locomotives are models of those used by the TVR, with the exception of the colliery area where some industrial shunters are used. The majority of TVR locomotives were tank engines and you will be able to see the following classes in use on the line - O3, U1 and M - the exception being the 'K' class tender locomotive which we use for mineral work.

Coaching stock is TVR, with a couple of other Welsh company vehicles used to show what is available. The wagons serving the colliery would, in most cases, be of one owner, but for show purposes it's nice to see a variety. The general wagons cover most of the Welsh Companies as well as some of those from across the border!

A list of all the rolling stock and who manufactured them will be at the end of the article for those who require more information.

A general view of Pistyll Graig Ddu.

A TVR M Class 0-6-2T arrives at Pistyll Graig Ddu with a passenger train including a refrigerator van.

TVR Locomotives

Nos.	Class	Notes
7, 130	A	Dragon Models (ex-D Mundy)
11	-	Scratch-built steam railmotor
15	M	Scratch-built
17	K	Dragon Models
30	U1	Scratch-built
57, 141	O3	Scratch-built
91	V	Dragon Models etch
93	O3	Scratch-built
767	S	Agenoria

Industrial Locomotives

Corwynt	Crane Tank	Roxey Mouldings
Tyniad	S&D Models	

TVR Coaching Stock

Auto coach	Scratch-built
Four-wheel composite	Scratch-built
Four-wheel third	Scratch-built from etches
Four-wheel brake third	Scratch-built from etches
Four-wheel full brake	Scratch-built from etches
Carriage Truck	Dragon Models/D Mundy
Horse Box	Dragon Models/D Mundy
Bogie Composite	D Mundy etch
TVR Brake vans	D Mundy Kits/Dragon Models

Other passenger stock and fitted vehicles by PC Models and Slater's. General goods vehicles for TVR and Cambrian by Dragon Models. Other goods vehicles from Slater's, Cooper Craft, Connoisseur Models and scratch-built.

A TVR bogie bolster loaded with timber stands outside the goods shed.

PYSTYLL CRAIG DDU TRACK PLAN

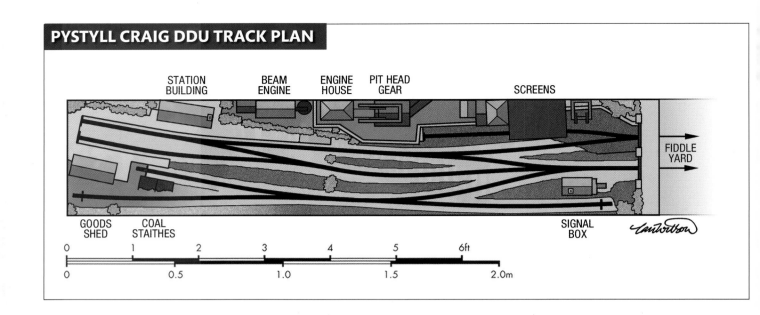

STATION BUILDING   BEAM ENGINE   ENGINE HOUSE   PIT HEAD GEAR   SCREENS   FIDDLE YARD

GOODS SHED   COAL STAITHES   SIGNAL BOX

| 0 | 1 | 2 | 3 | 4 | 5 | 6ft |
| 0 | 0.5 | 1.0 | 1.5 | 2.0m |

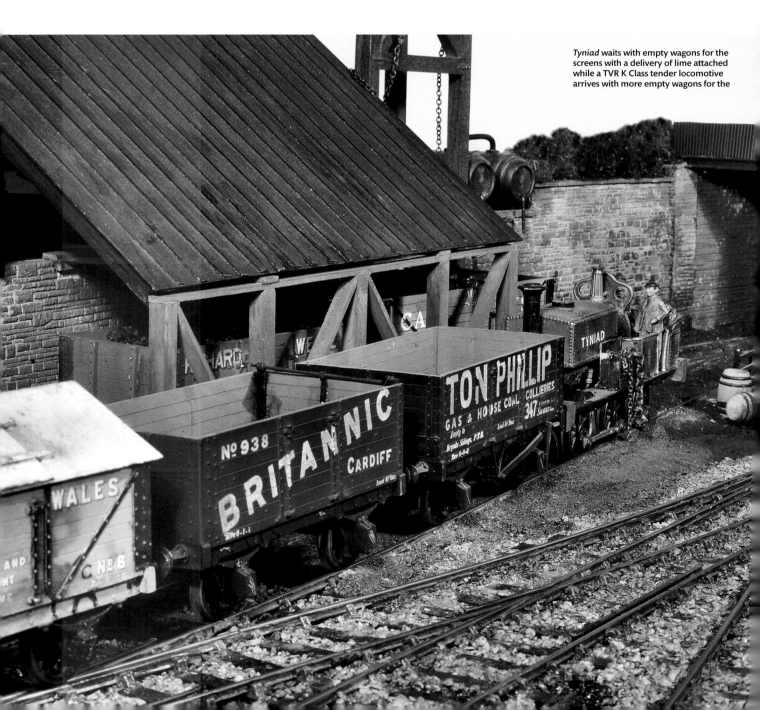

Tyniad waits with empty wagons for the screens with a delivery of lime attached while a TVR K Class tender locomotive arrives with more empty wagons for the

TVR 03 Class No.93 arrives with a goods train while an S Class 244 waits below the pit head winding house.

Power supply

Power to the layout is *via* a couple of multi-voltage transformers plus a couple of Gaugemaster power controllers and hand-held units. As previously mentioned, the point motors are positioned on the back edge of the baseboard for easy access and all of the cabling is against the edge,

The station area is split over the two baseboards and we decided that each board would have its own panel for points and section switches built in, reducing any additional wiring across the baseboard joint. **BRM**

USEFUL ADDRESSES

Agenoria
www.agenoria0gauge.com

Connoisseur Models
Tel: 01544 318263
www.jimmcgeown.com

Dragon Models
Tel: 02920 531246
email: chrisbasten@fsmail.net

Roxey Mouldings
www.roxeymouldings.co.uk

Crane tank *Corwynt* awaits the next raft of empty coal wagons for the screens. The screens are based on Bwlfa Dare Pit Screens c.1888.

Looking down on the 'Caley Single' and the 'Jones Goods' from the lofty height of the G&SWR tank prior to the opening of the museum.

Revolutionary Riverside

Richard Wilson visits Glasgow's exciting and radical new transport museum. *Photography by the author.*

North British-built South African Railways Class 15F 4-8-2 No.3007.

Wednesday June 1, 2011 saw an early morning stroll along the north bank of the Clyde in Glasgow from the Central Station down to the all-new Riverside site for the press preview of the city's superb new transport museum.

Long overdue expansion, it was decided to build a new museum on a high-profile site rather than rebuild or remodel the existing Museum of Transport in Kelvin Hall, which had opened in 1988 having been the exhibition and conference centre for the city prior to the opening of the Scottish Exhibition & Conference Centre which is just down river from the new museum.

Previously in industrial use, the land for the museum was donated by Glasgow Harbour as part of the long-term waterfront regeneration. The Riverside Museum Appeal was set up to raise £5 million towards the overall cost and so far over £4.5 million has been raised. More than 3,000 have donated so far and donations can still

be made by visiting the website or calling 0141 276 9515. In addition to the appeal, Glasgow City Council supplied funding of £47.4 million and the Heritage Lottery Fund £21.6 million.

The City Council wanted to employ an architect who could challenge the preconceptions of a transport museum and so appointed Zaha Hadid, who had, until then, not built significantly in the UK. Hadid's building is extremely radical, with a striking façade and an open, fluid design which cannot fail to get attention. The shape of the museum means that all the interior space is uncluttered by supports or columns and maximum use has been made of natural light.

Displays
All displays in the museum follow certain themes. As well as the Main Street which covers the period 1895-1930, there are two other street displays for the periods 1930-60 and 1960 to the 1980s.

The Riverside Museum
100 Pointhouse Place,
North Glasgow G3 8RS
Tel: 0141 287 2729
Email: riverside@glasgowlife.org.uk
www.glasgowmuseums.com/riverside

Open
Monday - Thursday and Saturday
10.00 am - 5.00 pm
Sunday
11.00 am - 5.00 pm
Admission free (except Tall Ship)
Pedestrian access is via the River
Clyde walkway from the SECC or a six-minute walk from Partick Rail, Bus and Underground Interchange. Visitors by car can use the slip road from the Clydeside Expressway. There is a car park for 330 cars outside the museum.

HR 'Jones Goods' 4-6-0 No.103, surely the most handsome goods loco ever built?

The largest object in the museum is South African Railways Class 15F 4-8-2 locomotive No.3007, built by the North British Locomotive Company between 1938-1948 at its Queen's Park Works in Polmadie, Glasgow as one of a fleet of 204. Used widely across SAR, including the famous 'Blue Train' from Johannesburg to Cape Town, this particular locomotive was withdrawn in 1988 following an accident the previous year and sat awaiting scrapping until 2006. Glasgow Museum, sensing the loco's importance, purchased it from the South African Government and it was transported back to the UK.

All the railway locomotives originally at the Kelvin Hall site, together with a selection of Glasgow Underground stock and artefacts have also been transported to the new site, where their innovative and open display makes them considerably more accessible than previously, while still retaining a sense of the radical. Indeed a Glasgow & South Western Railway tank has been positioned as if it is bursting through a first floor wall. Dedicated digital supporting displays in various languages give more information and stories behind the exhibits. BRM

NBR 'Glen' No.256 *Glen Douglas*.

Original Glasgow Subway entrance.

The most modern of Glasgow's trams, 1952 Cunarder Car No.1392.

Glagow Underground trailer car No.4 of 1896, when the railway was still cable hauled.